W9-AEC-094

ARAB INTELLECTUALS AND THE WEST:
The Formative Years, 1875–1914

Unto my children will I make amends for being the child of my fathers: and unto all the future—for *this* present day!

NIETZSCHE

ARAB INTELLECTUALS AND THE WEST:

The Formative Years, 1875–1914

HISHAM SHARABI
Professor of History
Georgetown University

Published in cooperation with The Middle East Institute

The Johns Hopkins Press

Baltimore and London

By the same author

A Handbook of the Contemporary Middle East (1956)
Governments and Politics of the Middle East in the 20th Century (1962)
Nationalism and Revolution in the Arab World (1966)
Palestine and Israel: The Lethal Dilemma (1969)
Palestine Guerillas: Their Credibility and Effectiveness (1970)

The Johns Hopkins Press, Baltimore, Maryland 21218
The Johns Hopkins Press Ltd., London

Library of Congress Catalog Card Number 78–108384

Standard Book Number 8018–1142–2

To my mother

Contents

Preface

Less than a century ago Arab society was still firmly tied to its medieval past; today it is still struggling to find its way to the modern world. The Arab Awakening, the term Arab intellectuals have used to describe the process of "modernization," was the product not of sudden spontaneous awareness, but of the challenge posed by the West on all levels of existence—social, political, economic, psychological—which began in the nineteenth century. This book is an attempt to examine this challenge and to analyze the Arab response to it on the level of intellectual consciousness.

The Arab Awakening involved a new sort of awareness. It brought about both new perceptions of the traditional heritage and attempts at adaptation to new conditions. In many ways it was a rending experience. On the social level it led to transformation and change involving loss of social cohesion; psychologically it reflected both widening self-consciousness and alienation.

As a modernizing process the Awakening unfolded under particular circumstances and passed through specific phases. The focus of this study is the first phase, which began in the late nineteenth century and continued into the early twentieth century (ca. 1875–1914). This phase was decisive: it set the tone for and profoundly influenced all subsequent developments. The second phase coincided with the interwar period, which began with the domination of the Arab world by the West and ended with the beginning of the Arab revolt against the West. The third phase, which corresponds to the post–World War II period, involves the political liberation of the Arab world from the West and its rejection of western bourgeois values and culture.

During the first phase, the impact of western civilization and the process of change which it generated were mostly confined to the Arab heartland—to Egypt and the Fertile Crescent.[1] Here the experience of social change has its deepest roots. After World War I modernization began to spread to other parts of the Arab world;

---

[1] The area between the head of the Persian Gulf and the Mediterranean.

shortly after the end of World War II it had penetrated into the Arab world's most detached regions—Saudi Arabia, Libya, Yemen, and the Persian Gulf sheikhdoms.

In this study I have tried to analyze the change from the standpoint of intellectual history. I have viewed the intellectuals of this period not through their "contributions," but in terms of their roles as commentators on and interpreters of their generation's experience. Thus the investigation stresses the conditions under which communication and conflict occurred and the forms in which these were expressed. For this reason I have put special emphasis on the social and psychological determinants of ideas.

In this kind of study, understanding is furthered more by the use of sociological and psychological analysis than by a descriptive approach. There is much to be said for this type of analysis, which the Germans (e.g., Max Scheler and Karl Mannheim) have called the sociology of knowledge. Indeed, without this perspective it probably would have been impossible to bring into focus many of the problems and relationships which give this study its special interest. It is my hope that this contribution will prove valuable not only to students of Arab society and culture in particular and students of intellectual history in general, but also to all those interested in the problems of modernization. The distinctive aspect of this study lies precisely in the effort to understand social change in terms of its relation to the explicit content of contemporary consciousness.

I wish to acknowledge my indebtedness to Albert Hourani, whose pioneering work, *Arabic Thought in the Liberal Age, 1798–1939,* is an indispensable reference to any study of modern Arab intellectual history. I should like to express my gratitude to the Social Science Research Council and to the John Simon Guggenheim Memorial Foundation for their generous support during the academic year 1963–64, the summer of 1965, and most of the calendar year 1967. I am grateful to Georgetown University for granting me leave from my regular academic duties to complete this book. And I wish to thank Mrs. Barbara Miller, of The Johns Hopkins Press, for her editorial assistance.

Washington, D.C.   H.B.S.
July 1969

ARAB INTELLECTUALS AND THE WEST:
The Formative Years, 1875–1914

Chapter I. The Emergence of the Arab Intelligentsia

"Are intellectuals an autonomous and independent social class," asked Antonio Gramsci, "or does every social class have its own specialized category of intellectuals?"[1] This question is central to this study, though in the social context with which I am concerned it can have no simple or complete answer. As Gramsci points out, the various forms taken by the historical process determine the growth of the different categories of intellectuals as well as the nature of their relations. Thus my analysis focuses on the social setting from which the intellectuals of this epoch emerged and the type of consciousness they possessed. The dependence of intellectuals on classes, or their development as autonomous groups detached from class loyalties, are problems which we will encounter. But this must take place against the background of a system of stratification that was still at a nascent stage of development when only the vaguest notion of class consciousness presented itself. Before examining specific relations it is necessary to outline the essential features of the concrete framework in which social relations in general presented themselves during this formative stage of the Arab Awakening.

First, it must be kept in mind that the social and economic ambience for the intellectuals of this period was essentially that of an agricultural, traditional, premodern society. Social forms and values and the predominant modes of production were basically the same as those prevailing in medieval times—with only minor exceptions in urban areas.

In the late nineteenth century, society in the Fertile Crescent and Egypt was basically rural. The bulk of the peasantry, particularly in the Fertile Crescent, lived under semifeudal conditions, ravaged by nature and exploited by marauding bedouin and occasional tax collectors. Communications were exceedingly primitive, and law and order were nonexistent in wide areas. The kinship system, which was based on family and tribe, constituted the basis of social organization. In the Fertile Crescent, a tribal ethos, deriving from the culture of the

[1] Antonio Gramsci, "The Formation of Intellectuals," *The Prince and Other Writings* (New York, 1968), p. 118.

desert, dominated fundamental impulses and behavior; in Egypt the dominant values were those of a settled, harmonious peasant culture. Society in the Fertile Crescent was heterogeneous and divided, with deep sectarian, ethnic, and linguistic cleavages; in Egypt it was homogeneous, peaceable, and cohesive.

Urban life was then at its inception. The towns were entering into their first period of expansion since the Middle Ages. In the growing towns of the Fertile Crescent, the dominant social elements were the aristocratic families, the representatives of the central government (the higher officials of the bureaucracy and the army), and the religious hierarchy. The mercantile class was making its appearance as commerce revived and the transportation system improved. In Egypt urban society was a simple two-segment structure: a high society, composed of the wealthy Turkish aristocracy and the European commercial bourgeoisie (including Jews and Levantines), and the "native" Egyptian population, a colonized people in the classical sense of the term.

The rise of the intellectuals and the elaboration of ideological functions must be seen as a manifestation of the process of education and enlightenment brought about by increasing contact with Europe. This was associated with the transformation of the political power of the aristocratic families and urbanized feudal chiefs, the rise of a mercantile class, and the disintegration of Ottoman hegemony with the corresponding extension of European domination. With the introduction of new values the unity of the old social order began to dissolve. For the newly educated, the gap between traditional norms and actual conduct grew wider, setting a pattern which continued to broaden as enlightenment and education spread. Naturally, the break with traditional values was accompanied by a corresponding break with tradition-bound society. The educated generation became alienated from the rest of the population at the same time and to the same degree that it became impregnated with the new culture. The process of enlightenment on the level of consciousness therefore involved a process of social and cultural estrangement.

As the intellectuals congealed into distinct groups according to their social origin and political and cultural orientations, each group tended to conceive of itself in terms of a specific cultural-political frame of reference. Generally speaking, the Christian intellectuals, who were the most strongly oriented toward European culture and values, tended to see themselves in terms of the values and ideals of the European bourgeoisie. The Muslim intellectuals, "conservatives," "reformists," as well as "secularists," regarded themselves in terms of opposition to European culture and domination. Whether or not they were well-disposed toward the established order in Egypt and the Ottoman Empire, they conceived of themselves as playing leadership roles in their own social milieus; and to them Ottomanism, Islam, and nationalism constituted basic, if often mutually exclusive, terms of reference. Together as a social category Christian and Muslim intellectuals traced, in their attitude, behavior, and the scope of their activities, the basic features which would later characterize the intelligentsia of the national bourgeoisie of nonwestern countries passing through the precapitalist stage of development. In their basic responses (including the negative ones) they echoed the dominant themes and ideas of the ruling and dominant social strata. In its purview the mass of the population figured hardly at all; for all practical purposes the masses were politically, socially, and intellectually nonexistent.

Composition of the Intelligentsia

Not since the high Middle Ages had an educated elite arisen in the Arab world that was distinctly separate from the closed religious stratum of the *ulema,*[2] who for generations had monopolized learning and intellectual activity. The impact of education and of the new ideas slowly but inexorably broke this monopoly; by the end of the nineteenth century a new intelligentsia had emerged in which the *ulema* (as well as the Arab Christian clergy) were but one of the participating groups. The dawning of critical consciousness brought about the disintegration of the old system of thought: the habit of a single way of thinking began to disappear, fixed categories to crumble, and divergent modes of thought to emerge.

My concern is to analyze the reaction of this new stratum to the mounting challenge of the West. I shall treat the Arab intellectuals as witnesses of the process of change and as participants in the Awakening. It was in their ideas and in their political attitudes that the challenge of the West was most clearly reflected. Their response, to be properly understood, should be analyzed not merely in terms of its theoretical content but in the light of the social reality which gave it particular form, the specific conditions which motivated it, and the experiences to which it gave expression.

The intellectuals did not constitute a closed group. Indeed, they were more often than not internally diversified and adhered to positions that were often opposed to one another. The common denomi-

[2] Plural of *'alim,* learned in the religious sciences; hence, a member of the "clergy."

nator that characterized many of them was the education to which they were exposed and the intellectual awareness it bestowed upon them. This became progressively more distinctive as the gulf between the educated and uneducated widened and as the number of the educated increased and their importance spread. The new education gave the literate groups not only a common language and a common intellectual experience but it also tended to cut them off psychologically from the older generation, on the one hand, and from the undifferentiated masses, on the other.

The vocations which these intellectuals—now using the term in its widest sense to include the *ulema,* reformists as well as conservatives —took up were as varied as their social origins and individual orientations. Certain vocations, however, tended to predominate: the religious institution, the army, teaching, journalism, and law. On the whole, the emerging educated generation found it difficult to fit into the existing administrative and political structures, though many of its members sought employment in the civil service.

In the Fertile Crescent during Abdul Hamid's reign (1876–1908), the more vociferous intellectuals were silenced by patronage or intimidation. In Egypt under British occupation the gulf between the foreign-dominated administration and the indigenous intelligentsia precluded any kind of normal relationship: suspicion and hostility marked the Egyptian attitude; detachment and coolness characterized that of the ruling circles. Many of the leading members of the intelligentsia in both Egypt and the Fertile Crescent were at one time or another forced to leave their countries for political or economic reasons. They traveled in various parts of the Ottoman Empire and Europe: Syrians escaped to Egypt, and Egyptians took refuge in Constantinople, and many sooner or later found themselves in Paris, London, or Geneva.

All intellectuals discussed here belonged to the "vocational intelligentsia" (to use Carl Mannheim's term), that is, those whose roles as intellectuals were lifelong careers.[3] The vocational intellectuals may be grouped according to their social and religious backgrounds as well as in terms of their political and intellectual orientations.

One grouping took the form of the traditional "circle" composed of

[3] Others may be placed in the category of "leisure time" intellectuals, or intellectuals of "a passing phase of life." A distinction, made by the late Lebanese literary critic and historian Maroun 'Abboud, is between those "who wrote in order to influence decision" and those "who simply engaged in fancy"; i.e., between those who addressed themselves to concrete social problems and those who confined themselves to literary subjects. *Ruwwad al-nahda al-haditha* [Pioneers of the Arab Renaissance] (Beirut, 1952), p. 164.

a number of disciples grouped around an eminent leader. The best example of this type of group was that formed around Jamal al-Din al-Afghani (1839–97) in Cairo in the 1870s. Equally important was the circle later formed by Afghani's leading disciple, Muhammad 'Abdu (1849–1905), some of whose members became leading figures in Egypt's political and intellectual life. In Syria the most important circle was that formed around Shaykh Tahir al-Jaza'iri (1851–1920), who had as disciples virtually every Muslim intellectual to emerge in Damascus in the pre-World War I period. A wide variety of topics occupied attention in these groups, but the central themes were religious and political: how to bring about the revival of Islam; how to deal with the threat of European civilization; how to strengthen ties between the nations of the Muslim world; and how to bring about pan-Islamic unity.

Another sort of grouping emerged from the secularizing and western-oriented intellectuals in the offices of the journals and newspapers, which became the literary and political centers of the educated younger generation in Cairo, Beirut, Damascus, and Baghdad. Examples of this kind of nuclei were Bustani's *al-Jinan* in Beirut, Nimr and Sarruf's *al-Muqtataf,* Zaydan's *al-Hilal,* Rida's *al-Manar* in Cairo, Kurd 'Ali's *al-Muqtabis* in Damascus, and, to a lesser extent, Father Marie Anasthasius's *Lughat al-'Arab* in Baghdad. A small body of readers, occasional contributors, and hangers-on supported these centers by their moral, political, and, sometimes, financial backing. Interest among these groups centered mostly on philosophy, history, science, and literature.

A third type of group took the form of a literary society or club. Though more formally organized, the literary club was a looser gathering than those of the circles or periodicals. The literary club served primarily as a place for social gatherings and literary discussions. After the overthrow of Abdul Hamid in 1908, these clubs became more and more politically oriented and provided a breeding ground for nationalist agitation.

It was from such clubs that the fourth and most closely knit grouping emerged, the political secret societies. The secret societies arose exclusively in the Fertile Crescent. For the most part they were the result of impatience with slow administrative and political reform and the expression of growing Arab opposition to Ottoman domination. These underground groups included in their membership the bulk of the professional and educated elite of the rising Muslim generation. Most of these young men had belonged to the literary circles and to the clubs, where they had acquired their new social and political ideas. The secret societies differed from the rest of the groups in that their main preoccupation was nationalism. The real issues here were not Islam or modernism or science or literature, although these topics still drew much concern. The main concern was with practical politics, and it was in these societies that this generation of Arab intellectuals came closest to engaging in revolutionary action.

Though the underground phase did not lead to a definite political movement in the Fertile Crescent, it did serve as the groundwork for a number of political parties after World War I. In Egypt such parties had come into being much earlier, first in embryo form during the 'Urabi movement (1879–82, prior to the British occupation), later in full force during Mustafa Kamel's (1874–1908) leadership of the Nationalist Party.[4] For the Fertile Crescent the only political groups were founded in exile, in Cairo, Geneva, and Paris.[5] Though these parties were skeleton organizations, they nevertheless formed a new and distinct type of grouping, and they represented a new phase of political consciousness which was to reach its apex in the period between the two world wars.

Conservatives, Reformists, and Modernists

The response of the intellectuals to the challenge presented by the West assumed the familiar polarity between two broad outlooks: traditionalism and modernism. Modernism in this context is to be understood as a positive attitude toward innovation and change and toward western civilization generally; traditionalism is to be viewed as a negative attitude toward all types of innovation and toward the West. Modernism thus represents a dynamic outlook, essentially pragmatic and adaptable; traditionalism a static position, fundamentally passive and hardly able to react to external stimuli.

The traditionalism of the late nineteenth century was essentially reactionary in character. Its more articulate protagonists are what we have labeled the "conservative" intellectuals. The basic orientation of this traditionalism was historicist, to use the term in a purely descriptive sense; that is, it derived its inspiration and strength from a historically evolved tradition and in its intellectual attitude always assumed a backward-looking stance. For the traditionalist, the past, rather than the future, was the locus of the Golden Age. The past was restorable and one day would be restored. Conservative traditionalist

---

[4] See B. Aclietti, "Mustafa Kamel (1874–1908) foundatore del Partito Nazionalista egiziano," *Oriente Moderno*, vol. XXII (1942), pp. 305–17.

[5] By far the most important of these was *hizb al-la markaziyya al-'uthmani* [Party of Ottoman Decentralization].

thought, though it may not have wholeheartedly espoused the status quo, did not repudiate it. As the only concrete reality, the established order represented continuity and the only link with the past; it constituted the starting point of revival and the only basis on which to resist the European threat.

The modernist outlook, on the other hand, was forward-looking. All modernists repudiated the status quo and derived their central assumptions not from traditionalism but from European thought. The modernist outlook was fundamentally utopian in character: the Golden Age lay not in the past but in the future.

Between conservative traditionalism and progressive modernism there was a middle ground occupied by what may best be termed the reformist position. Reformism has often been referred to as Islamic modernism,[6] but reformism was modernizing only in a special sense and a limited degree. At heart, reformism was tradition-bound; its primary goal was to safeguard Islam and the institutional structures upholding it. As a revivalist movement, reformism was in fact not much more than enlightened conservatism, equipped with a more rational awareness of its situation and needs. The reformist position, in its fundamental premises and ultimate conclusions, opposed the secularization and "westernization" elements of social modernization more effectively than conservative traditionalism ever did precisely because it was more rational. But at the same time it opened the door for change within prescribed limits. Reformism was the movement of the younger liberal *ulema* who knew that Islam, to be properly defended, had to overcome its inertia and be revitalized. In this respect, they were modernizers of traditional Islam and they inevitably collided with the established traditional hierarchy. It is in this sense that the basic distinction between Muslim conservatives and Muslim reformers should be made.

Christian Westernizers and Muslim Secularists

It is easier to define Islamic conservatism and Islamic reformism than it is to define the position of the Christian westernizers and that of the Muslim secularists. The modernist position was represented by the two principal and essentially differing groups of intellectuals, which we are here designating as the "Christian westernizing" and "Muslim secularist" groups. Differentiation between the two types of intellectuals cannot always be clear-cut; the outlook and attitude of

---

[6] The term was coined by Charles Adams, *Islam and Modernism in Egypt* (London, 1933), and used by scholars in this broad, imprecise sense.

the one approximates those of the other. But despite similarities the ultimate foundations of each are different.

The distinctive characteristic of the Christian perspective lies in the fact that Christian intellectuals, despite individual differences, recognized and upheld values and goals that not merely derived from the West but served culturally to identify Arab Christians with the West. Here an essential otherness asserted itself in the Arab Christian position in relation to its Muslim environment. In contrast, Muslims with similar secularist persuasions remained, no matter how thorough their "westernization," essentially alien to the West; the Muslim secularist, while upholding western values and modern ideas, affirmed his separate Muslim identity.

This differentiation within the modernist wing of the Arab intelligentsia had a major influence on the intellectual evolution of the epoch. From the Christian standpoint modernization necessarily meant westernization (or Europeanization); social change could have only one model, European society. In this respect, however, radical opposition presented itself most strongly not between the Christian westernizing position and Muslim secularism, but between the former and Islamic conservatism. Yet between the two extremes there remained, as we shall see, surprisingly extensive areas of agreement, or at least of positive communication. This was in large part owing to the fact that Christian westernizers never carried their premises to the end nor allowed themselves fully to confront the problem of Islam or to attempt to reconcile it with the necessity for change. The Christian intellectuals were always aware that they represented only a minority of the society, that they could never speak for society as a whole.

This, probably as much as any other single factor, made them the most "unattached" (to use Alfred Weber's term) group within the Arab intelligentsia of this epoch. From this flowed two important consequences. First, the Christian intellectuals consciously limited their horizons to avoid conflict with Arab Muslim society: hence the many paradoxical aspects of development within Christian thought. Secondly, though theoretically the task of resolving the contradictions between the movements of modernity and tradition could have been carried out by the Christian intellectuals, practically the contradictions had to be faced and the task accomplished by Muslims and from within Islamic thought. Only Muslim secularism possessed the legitimacy to do this, which meant opposing Islamic conservatism on several levels.

The Muslim secularists were perhaps the most diverse in composition and outlook. Psychologically, they fluctuated in a wide arc between positions of extreme westernism and extreme conservatism. Belonging to the younger generation, however, they tended to assume increasingly modernist attitudes. Their emancipation from the traditionalism of their upbringing and early education was a product of familiarity with western ways and values, which they received with mixed enthusiasm and apprehension.

Probably owing to the peculiar experience of this generation, Muslim secularists seemed incapable of constructing a focused and coherent intellectual position. While Islamic reformism and Christian westernism may be reduced to fairly specific assumptions, Muslim secularism remained somewhat vague and diffuse in its outlook and values. Yet in certain important respects the Muslim secularists came close to forming a kind of synthesis, or connection, between the Christian westernizing intellectuals, the Islamic conservatives, and the reformist *ulema*. This synthesis showed itself primarily in the evolution within Muslim secularism of the spirit of nationalism, which tended as much toward the secular notion of Arabism (and Egyptian nationalism) as toward Islam and the Islamic heritage.

An especially significant trend developed within this broad movement of thought as the period drew to a close with the outbreak of World War I. Christian westernism and Muslim secularism began to move closer to one another as they adopted, especially after the formation of the secret societies and of political groups abroad, positions that reflected near identity of political views. Islamic conservatism and Islamic reformism, on the other hand, tended to move apart: one toward withdrawal from public ferment; the other toward more and more reconciliation with the status quo.[7]

The effort to modernize Arab society required two separate but complementary tasks: to make innovation legitimate and to demolish old intellectual and social forms. This process threatened an intellectual revolt of the first order. Not only was the old content of thought questioned, but the *way* of thinking was challenged. The newness in modernist thought was not just in fresh ideas, but in the manner in which ideas were formulated and joined together. The very categories of the mind seemed to undergo profound transformation: meaning began to be based on clearer and more palpable grounds; language appeared to gain in logic and transparency. A spirit of rebellion seemed to be born out of increasing lucidity.

[7] E.g., Afghani died while under Abdul Hamid's patronage in Constantinople; 'Abdu collaborated with the British administration in Egypt and in the last years of his life was Grand Mufti of Egypt.

Polarization of Thought

The polarization of thought accompanying this development crystallized in two types of mentality, each with its own set of values, ideas, and perspectives. The Christian westernizers and Muslim secularists represented together one type of mentality, and the Islamic conservatives and reformists the other. In most cases, the two outlooks were in very strong opposition; in others, they often tended to become disengaged, with each going its own way. As disengagement became more frequent, discussion became more and more tangential, and, on fundamental issues, the position of each seemed to drop out of the other's scope of vision.

Perhaps the best way to describe this polarity is to borrow Max Scheler's scheme of tabulation.[8]

Islamic Conservatism and Islamic Reformism (tradition-based thought)	*Christian Westernism and Muslim Secularism* (modern-oriented thought)
Tendency to look backward	Tendency to look forward
Salaf[9]	Progress
Dogmatism	Pragmatism
Authority	Science
Reality-transcending doctrine	"Scientific" doctrine
"Teleological orientation of thought"	"Materialistic orientation of thought"
Static views of social values	Dynamic views of social values
Permanence of truth	Relativism of truth

Although Islamic reformists (in contrast to Islamic conservatives) were open to the values and achievements of modern science, they never really attempted to work out a systematic accommodation to it. Mostly they satisfied themselves with verbal compromises, tending always toward a defensive or apologetic stance. Instead of reformulating their assumptions in modern terms (as the leading reformists attempt), they chose to follow traditional methods of rationalization. Propaganda and polemics rather than criticism and analysis dominated their approach.

Christian westernizers and Muslim secularists, on the other hand, sought with varying degrees of success to adjust their conceptions of reality to the new forms of knowledge. Released to a certain extent from traditional moorings, they were unencumbered, as Islamic re-

---

[8] *Die Wissenformen und die Gesellschaft* (Leipzig, 1926), pp. 204–5.
[9] Literally, "predecessors."

formists always were encumbered, by commitments to absolute positions. Justifications could thus take cultural (i.e., secular) rather than
religious forms. They tended to justify modernizing attitudes in terms
of historical interpretations—which appeared harmless from the point
of view of orthodoxy but which carried within them implications
going far beyond orthodox positions.

Let us now turn to the social situation and background of each of
the three leading groups of Arab intellectuals—the *ulema* (conservatives and reformists), the westernizing Christians, and the Muslim
secularists—and see if and how the social situation of each group had
any relevance to its psychological orientation and mode of thought.

The Ulema

In Egypt the *ulema* belonged to the lower classes; they came
mostly from the villages and the poorer strata of urban society. In the
Fertile Crescent, however, a substantial number belonged to higher
economic strata; many came from well-known and established families. These differences in social origin influenced the roles of the
ulema in their respective societies.

But in both the Fertile Crescent and Egypt this group was formed
intellectually by essentially the same type of training and education,
which in the nineteenth century had changed little since the days of
al-Ghazzali (d. 1111). This rested on four principal pivots, the
Qur'an, the *hadith*, Islamic law, and Arabic grammar; all other
subjects were directly or indirectly related to these. Training in the
traditional sciences automatically equipped the *ulema* with a profes-
sion and the power to earn a living; it also bestowed upon them a
certain social function and status in society. The *ulema* as a social
group constituted, together with the army and the bureaucracy, one of
the most important hierarchies in society.

The role of the *ulema* encompassed a wide range of functions. In
the villages and among the urban poor they were leaders of the
community. They performed most of the important duties: they acted
as judges, provided religious and political guidance on Friday, educated the young, performed marriages, and laid the dead to rest. They
represented the force of order and stability and served as the strongest supporters of the status quo. The upper strata of the *ulema* played
an important part in government; some wielded significant power as
leaders of *sufi tariqas* (religious brotherhoods).

The *ulema* naturally tended to be politically and intellectually
conservative. Their political conservatism had its roots in the theological premises of traditional Islam. Man's relationship to God was

viewed basically in terms of a master-slave relationship. The same
relationship reflected itself in the subordination of subjects to their
ruler. There was no question, from the standpoint of the *ulema,* as to
the sultan's (or khedive's) absolute power over his subjects. Ideas of
constitutional government and parliamentary democracy were regarded with suspicion: They not only violated the prescriptions of the
Law but were instruments designed to bring about the collapse of
Islam's hegemony.

As long as official orthodoxy was politically strong the position of
the *ulema* remained straightforward and uncompromising; the caliphate embodied all temporal power and was the source of all legitimacy in society and the state. The person of the caliph was seen in
two ways: as the successor of Muhammad, the caliph was *Imam*
(head) of the community of the faithful throughout *dar al-Islam*
(Muslim world); he was also the sultan and *padishah* of the Ottoman
Empire. He was the "shadow of God on earth" who derived his
sovereignty not from the people but directly from God. The people
(the *ra'iyya,* literally, flock), whose duty was absolute submission
(*islam*) to God, were bound to equally unqualified submission to the
caliph. The *ulema* thus adhered to a theory of absolutism which
resembled not so much the European theory of the divine right of
kings as the theory elaborated by the Russian Orthodox Church to
justify tsarist absolutism. As in Russia, the religious institution accepted complete subordination to the ruling institution in return for
the latter's recognition of its rights and privileges in the social order.

The *ulema* as a class preserved its unity of outlook by emphasizing
the dogmatic foundations of social truth. The psychological attitude
that resulted from this position was attuned to the timeless mode of
life of the *ra'iyya.* So long as the rhythm of life remained undisturbed,
individuals and groups accepted themselves and their conditions without question or protest. The established method of confronting the
hazards of existence and the way of transmitting inherited wisdom
contributed to the suppression of individuality and the inhibition of
independent self-awareness. This attitude preserved a mode of
thought that offered no possibility of seeing the same thing from more
than one point of view; the traditional frame of reference was kept at
the center of collective consciousness. The *ulema* instinctively knew
that, once the principle of questioning was admitted, unity of outlook,
and with it both inner and social stability, would inevitably be shat-
tered. This is why the majority of them vehemently opposed the new
way of thought advocated by the reformers and modernizers. This
position was also consistent with their interests as a class. Any kind of

fundamental reformulation of traditional principles or of ways of thinking about doctrinal problems involved not merely the introduction of dangerous innovation but also the adoption of attitudes that were bound to go counter to the values and approach of Islamic orthodoxy. Thus the movement of Islamic reform, as spearheaded by Afghani and 'Abdu, contributed, to the extent that it was successful, to the disintegration of the *ulema*'s intellectual system and consequently to the disintegration of their position and power in society.

Harassed not only by the forces of change from without but also by the efforts of the reforming *ulema* from within, the conservative *ulema* were pushed to extreme positions. Politically this found its strongest expression in the concept of pan-Islamism, which opposed the secular concept of nationalism. Thus Muslims were brothers regardless of national affiliation; there was no difference between Arab and Turk, Egyptian and Persian, Afghani and Indonesian. Pan-Islamism as envisioned by the conservatives referred to a Muslim *ummah* (community) encompassing the entire Muslim world from Morocco to central Asia and from the Mediterranean to Indonesia.[10]

In contrast to the reformists, the conservatives had no prominent spokesmen. Their ideological stand took the form not of intellectual expression, but of political orientation. The revival in the latter part of the nineteenth century of the caliphal prerogatives of the Ottoman sultanate constituted a decisive element of this orientation.

The inability of the conservative *ulema* to express their ideology in a systematic fashion was owing to their belief that there was nothing new to be said. All energy was directed toward reiterating in traditional terms the old tested truths. During this period a large body of work, now wholly forgotten, was put out by the conservative polemicists in which familiar themes and traditional topics were elaborated upon at great length. All of these eschewed with great care the treatment of any problem that smacked of "modernity."[11]

A typical example of conservative thought and style is provided by the pseudomystical treatises of Abu'l-Huda al-Siyadi (d. 1900?), for

[10] In this the reformists went along with the conservatives because they saw that Islam's political revival had its best chances for success in the context of a pan-Islamic movement. See Chapter III.

[11] For interesting comments on works by the conservative *ulema*, see the observations of a reformist member of the group, 'Abd al-Qadir al-Mughrabi, *Jamal al-Din al-Afghani: Dikriyat wa ahadith* [Conversations with Afghani and Recollections about Him] (Cairo, 1948), p. 13. For comments by an emancipated Muslim contemporary, see Salah al-Din al-Qasimi, *Atharuhu: safahat min tarikh al-nahda al-'arabiyya fi awa'il al-qarn al-'ishrin* [Collected Papers: Pages on the History of the Arab Renaissance in the Early Twentieth Century], ed. Muhib al-Din al-Khatib (Cairo, 1959), p. 8.

many years Abdul Hamid's famous chief adviser. Here we enter a truly medieval universe, tenuously linked to contemporary reality: things happen for no necessary reason; power, pure and undefined, pervades everything; man, in the grip of an omnipotent, mysterious force, is utterly helpless. All attempts at rational presentation are abandoned in advance, and an almost deliberate attempt to confuse and mystify is evident on every page.[12]

The conservative *ulema* expressed themselves in a language and style designed to screen the believer's mind from the realities of the workaday world. The concrete concerns of existence were banished, and a barrier was erected to maintain the divorce between the spoken language of every day and the formal "literary" Arabic of ritual and ceremony. Language in their hands became an emblem of status and an instrument of control. It served as a "distancing" agent which perpetuated their monopoly over esoteric knowledge and familiarity with sacred texts.

The tension between conservative and reformist *ulema,* however, never reached a breaking point. As we shall see, the reformist tenets remained firmly rooted in traditional grounds. The essential difference was that the reformists chose to formulate a rational response to the intellectual and political challenge of the West. In doing so they tried to transcend the formalism and inertia of the conservatives and accommodate modern civilization; the conservatives thought this would be impossible without succumbing to the West.

The Christian Intellectuals

A Christian Arab may seem like a contradiction in terms. The fact is, however, that the Christian Arab intellectuals played a central role in the Arab Awakening and left a lasting stamp on the movement of Arab modernization.

The decisive characteristic of all Christian intellectuals, which differentiated them from their fellow Muslim Arab intellectuals and which bestowed upon them a special role in the nineteenth-century renaissance, was the fact that they were, in a deep and real sense, outsiders in Muslim society.

To be a Maronite or a Greek Orthodox or a Protestant Arab immediately placed one in a negative relationship to his environment.

[12] Muhammad Rashed Rida (1865–1935), the disciple of 'Abdu and editor of *al-Manar,* wrote interesting reviews of works by Abu'l-Huda, *al-Haqiqa al-bahira fi asrar al-shari'a al-tahira* [The Dazzling Truths of the Secrets of the Sacred Law] and *Faraqan al-qulub* [Fear in the Heart]. See *al-Manar,* vol. IX (1916), pp. 309–11, 550–52.

Ottoman rule for the Christian Arab was—much more than it ever was for his fellow Muslim Arab—*foreign* rule. Christians aspired to be liberated one day by France, Britain, or some other European power. Except in Mount Lebanon and the city of Beirut, Christians in most areas constituted a minority. Under Ottoman rule, being Christian meant being oppressed. Any young Christian with some education had to break through barriers of discrimination and antagonism to make his way.

All Christian intellectuals had at least one thing in common, the wrenching experience of being uprooted. In Syria, Lebanon, and Palestine this movement took a distinct direction: from the villages to the larger cities, from the interior to the coast (primarily to Beirut), and from there across the sea to Egypt[13]—and later to Europe and America.[14]

The Christians emigrated to escape oppression and humiliation, but also for economic reasons. The Christians' motives for leaving, even when political considerations were present, were different from those of their Muslim counterparts. Between the Christian and the Muslim society, of which he was legally a part, there was no real or lasting bond. Obviously he could never develop the same kind of allegiance to the Ottoman caliphate as his Muslim compatriot. The only form of loyalty he knew expressed itself in nostalgia for his native village, in longing for his family, in the feeling of solidarity with members of his sect. The other form of loyalty, that based on the sentiment of nationalism, was late in emerging.[15]

These Christian intellectuals formed a fluid, detached social stratum. But their freedom, as well as their mental attitude, was condi-

[13] Since 1882 Egypt had been under British rule, thus affording the Christians more freedom than any other country within the Ottoman Empire.

[14] Paris was the "capital of freedom." E.g., Adib Ishaq (1856–85), when arriving in Paris in the late 1870s, expressed his feeling in these words: "I am now under the sky of justice, on the land of peace, among the people of liberty . . ." See Sami al-Dahnan, *Qudama' wa mu'asirun* [Ancients and Moderns] (Cairo, 1961), p. 207.

[15] In the early part of this period for a Christian to regard himself as an Arab and part of the Arab nation was rather uncommon. 'Abd al-Masih al-Antaki (1874–1922), a Greek Orthodox Christian and a man of letters, describes how he came to feel himself an Arab: "I grew up in Aleppo in a social environment full of bigotry and ignorance. As luck would have it our house was on a street inhabited mostly by Arabs of the Muslim faith. Their kind treatment and neighborly spirit were so different from what I had been told about Muslims by my fellow Christians. I grew up with views altogether different from those held by other Christians about this noble people. When I reached manhood I realized that . . . we were all Arabs sharing one Arab homeland." See Sami al-Kayyali, *al-Adab al-mu'asir fi suriya* [Modern Syrian Literature: 1850–1950] (Cairo, 1959), p. 81.

tioned by the circumstances under which they grew and made their living. In their generally precarious mode of existence they tended to place a high premium on the values of survival and the virtues associated with it. A few Christians joined the Ottoman bureaucracy or traveled to Egypt; others went into business or journalism or emigrated to the New World. Some Maronites and Greek Orthodox Christians converted, out of opportunism or genuine faith, to Protestantism and worked with Protestant missionaries as teachers, translators, and administrators.

The mental and psychological outlook of these Christians was sharply different from that of the established and firmly rooted Muslims of the same generation. The Christian, uprooted and on his own, not only gained distance from his traditional background but plunged into a wholly different world of life and experience. The Christian simply had to fall back on his own resources, develop his own powers, and so try to face the world on its own terms. His life was an enterprise, shaped by the challenges with which existence presented him.

In a way it was inevitable for the educated and self-aware Christian Arab to see life and society from a special angle. It was impossible, for example, to maintain for long strong commitments to norms and values held by the society around him; new values—success, achievement, initiative, and competitiveness—which were alien to his environment were born out of the actions and decisions of his new mode of life.

A distinctive characteristic of the Christian's attitude, and another product of his existential situation, was a strong tendency toward rationalism. This expressed itself in his eager acceptance of the scientific and social theories of the day. It was somewhat easier for the unattached Christian intellectuals to abandon traditional conceptions and to adopt modern views than it was for the young educated Muslims. There were no mental and social restrictions for the Christians such as those which bound the rising Muslim intellectuals.

The Christians' rationalistic tendencies contained the seeds of rebellion against all forms of absolutist, other-worldly thought. In this respect, the Christian intellectuals, especially the outspoken journalists and publicists, far from being passive observers, were intellectual rebels who played an important role in radicalizing contemporary thought. No wonder that, to the practicing Muslim and more specifically to the *ulema,* these Christian intellectuals appeared not as simple innovators but as corrupters of tradition and traditional values. In what they said and, equally important, in the manner in which they said it, there was something more serious than a violation of a practice. There was present a trespassing, an element of heresy, an incipient revolt.

The educated Christians were wholeheartedly predisposed to adopt the modern civilization of Europe. If nothing else, their social fluidity and corresponding mode of response and thought naturally favored the innovating impulse and the hungry assimilation of the new ideas coming from the West. They constituted the natural vanguard of change, for they formed the stratum most readily able to respond to the new forces and to adapt them to their needs. Indeed, it was in being the interpreters of the West and purveyors of its values that the Christian Arab intellectuals discharged their most important function in Muslim Arab society.[16]

The distinctive nature of the Christian approach to the Arab heritage lay in its secular orientation. Through Christian eyes Arabic literature appeared in a new and fresh light which made possible its analysis and appreciation in terms of aesthetic and literary criteria. The religious Islamic element was consciously put aside; interest focused on structure and style. The number of grammatical works and poems published by Christian writers during this period attest to this typically Christian interest. Indeed, one can say that the Arabic language was modernized in the nineteenth century under the influence of two main groups: the Christian literati of the Fertile Crescent (mainly Lebanon) and the Egyptian translators of European works.

Literature took a markedly humanistic direction as a result of the Christians' contribution. The influence of European literature on the minds and tastes of Christian intellectuals constituted an important factor in this process. It must be kept in mind that for some time the Christians were the primary recipients of western education and were the first to travel frequently to Europe and to become familiar with European culture at first hand. Because of all this, the influences that molded and oriented the emerging literary imagination were predominantly western in character.

The secularization of Arabic literature thus would never have come about solely by means of the movement of translation from European works. The distinctive Christian contribution lay in transforming from the inside, both emotionally and intellectually, the literary sensibility and creation. This achievement is reflected above all in the shift from a transcendentally dominated perspective to one in which man and his condition begin to occupy a central position. Literature acquired

[16] See Hisham Sharabi, "Die arabischen Intellecktuellen im 19. Jahrhundert," *Bustan*, vol. VII (1966), pp. 12–13.

the potential of becoming the medium of social and aesthetic awareness after having been exclusively the vehicle of ritual and ceremony.

Thanks to the Christian intellectuals the forms and values of a new
consciousness emerged alongside a budding humanistic secularism.
From the existential standpoint of unattachment there grew a special
appreciation for the value of individuality. On the social and political
levels libertarian ideology exerted a strong appeal.

In the course of the evolution of social and political awareness
among the Christian writers there gradually emerged the idea of
secular nationalism. From the Christian standpoint the only viable
form of political organization would naturally be based on the national rather than the religious principle of community. The idea of
the theocratic state (on which Ottoman society was based) was not
only incompatible with "reason" and "progress" and the modern
world but went counter to the new consciousness of Arab history and
identity. Arabism presented itself as the doctrine of the new political
awareness. It made possible the crucial distinction between Turk and
Arab without reference to religion. What this Christian-inspired feeling demonstrated with increasing clarity was that a common religion
did not necessarily make for a common destiny, that Arabism expressed interests and loyalties that went beyond those of religion.
Arabism stood opposed to Ottomanism and, by one remove, to
pan-Islamism.

Yet the full implications of this line of reasoning were slow in being
drawn. For many educated Christians, as for most Muslim intellectuals, it seemed possible to build a secular national society within the
framework of the Ottoman Empire under some form of political and
administrative decentralization. The dual monarchy of Austro-Hun-
gary served as a convincing example. These practical political considerations provided perhaps the strongest ground for cooperation between the Christian westernizing intellectuals and the educated
Muslim elite.

The Muslim Secularist Elite

The term "Muslim secularist," as we have used it so far, is only a
label like "Islamic reformist" and "Christian westernizer." The word
"secularism" should not be taken in its literal meaning. It is intended
to distinguish those Muslim intellectuals who were not directly involved in the movement of Islamic revival from those who were
involved, namely, the reformist *ulema*. This group included individuals who differed considerably in their attitudes toward the religious
issue but who nevertheless had certain broad characteristics in com-

mon that set them apart from both the *ulema* and the Christian intellectuals. Within this group there was perhaps a wider range of variation than in the other two groups. As already mentioned, there were some who stood very close to the Islamic reformist position, others who came very close to the westernizing standpoint, and some who adhered more or less to a middle position. The distinctive outlook of this middle position may be regarded as the common denominator of the group as a whole.

The social background and education of the Muslim secularists gave them a special character. Whether they were in Egypt or in the Fertile Crescent, they belonged to the socially established urban strata. In Egypt there were many exceptions to this rule, but in Syria and Iraq the Muslim secularist elite came almost exclusively from the Muslim *Sunni* (upper middle class). The Egyptians as well as the Syrians and Iraqis were all exposed to more or less the same process of socialization: They experienced similar patterns of upbringing; they had the same value system; and they received the same type of education.

The influence of traditionalism was strongly felt in the early years of schooling, particularly in the *kuttab,* but also in the first years of elementary school as well. The Qur'an and the basic rudiments of the faith dominated early adolescence. Exposure to further education, particularly western-type education, constituted a later, drastic, formative experience. Higher education, on the college or professional levels, was pursued in Cairo, Beirut, Constantinople, or Paris. Members of this generation were the first Muslims to experience the systematic grafting of modern mental habits and outlook onto their traditional upbringing. With them began the alienation of the educated Muslim.

Still, in contrast with their Christian counterparts, these young Muslims felt secure in their environment. They were born into a world they viewed as their own. For members of their social class it held out the promise of privilege, wealth, and influence. The experience of uprootedness so typical of the Christian intellectual was foreign to the educated Muslim. Though members of this group experienced much mobility, movement was nearly always voluntary; the moments of exile were provisional. More important perhaps is the fact that the move from Damascus to Cairo, or from Cairo to Constantinople, did not constitute, as it often did for the Christian, a stage in emigration. In the Ottoman Empire and Egypt the Muslim always found himself within the ambit of a known and familiar world. The Muslim of "good family" from Syria or Iraq, for example, was never a foreigner in Egypt in the same sense that an Arab Christian from the same countries was.[17] For the Muslim, exile from the parental home was more of a temporary excursion; it was not a forced plunge into the unknown. Except in rare cases the Muslim always came back; the Christian almost never did.

These Muslim secularists were strongly influenced in their attitude toward economic activity by their social position and experience. Even when educated, the Muslim never seemed strongly driven, as his Christian colleague constantly was, by the economic impulse. He appeared to be protected by family ties and shielded from the threat of penury by inherited position. He rarely raised his sights above the condition into which he was born, which usually was high enough, and his tastes, even after exposure to the temptations of Europe, seemed to remain unchanged. He appeared incapable of adapting himself to the world of money and business. The bourgeois world with its calculatory and negotiable values remained basically foreign to him, and, it would seem, not quite comprehensible. The entrepreneurial spirit that fired the Christian left him untouched; it had to await the emergence of another Muslim generation to find expression in his class. As a result he failed to acquire the habits and qualities of character that animated the Economic Man of the modern age. He regarded work from the standpoint of status and prestige, not from that of profit and success. It is not surprising that his preference lay in government service, the army, and law, rather than in commerce or industry.

Not surprisingly, despite close similarity of attitude with regard to social and political problems, there were distinct differences between the basic positions of Muslim secularism and Christian westernism. Beneath practical agreement on specific issues and sincere cooperation in large areas of endeavor, there always remained profound differences in psychological attitude, taste, basic interests, and goals.

While the Muslim was confident and relaxed in his social bearing, the Christian was usually beset with anxiety, always on the move. The Muslim presented the image of the self-assured insider, the Christian that of the self-conscious outsider. The former saw himself as master in his own house, the latter as something of an alien. It is in this light that, from the Christian standpoint, there was no valid type of

---

[17] Indeed, Christians of Syrian origin constituted part of the foreign (European) community in Egypt. With the Egyptianization of the country's economic structure in the 1950s, most of the wealthier descendants of Syrian Christians were forced to leave the country along with Greeks, Italians, and other foreign residents.

social or political action except that which brought about significant transformation of man and society.

Obviously, the Muslim secularist could never be as truly secular as the Christian westernizer. Although he did not allow his approach to be dominated by the religious point of view, he was not at all ready to engage in serious religious criticism. His secularist tendency stopped at the point where he became unwilling to deal with social and political reform independently of religious considerations. True, even Muslims with strong religious feelings implicitly accepted the separation of state and church; however, they never drew the final and necessary conclusion from this position.

The fundamental difference in this respect between Muslim secularism and Christian westernism may be seen in the former's espousal of a mild *reformist* policy and the latter's policy of radical transformation. Though there were no true revolutionaries before 1914, the intellectual foundations of rebellion were being established at that time and were being expressed much more forcefully by the Christian than by the Muslim intellectuals. The Muslim secularist writers and publicists viewed the existing state of affairs "critically" in order to improve it. They viewed the existing social order, as did their fathers, in its historical perspective—the product of a process which had its ultimate origin and meaning in Islam and Arab society. Thus whatever could be accomplished in social and political reform was to be achieved from within the existing order and in terms of the Arab and Islamic cultural framework. This position, however, allowed significant variations in political attitude among this generation of Muslim secularists. Some felt that the only solution for the social and political crisis was to rally around the Ottoman caliphate and to support pan-Islamism. Others insisted that the only way was to destroy Ottoman tyranny and to restore the caliphate to the Arabs. Still others believed the best solution was a compromise between Arab ambitions and Ottoman integrity—autonomy within a framework of decentralization.

For the Christian westernizers, reform signified radical transformation according to the European model, but for the conservatives, if not the reformists, westernization was regarded as the beginning of the end of Islam. While the Christians wished to open up completely the avenues of change, the religiously oriented Muslims wished for their total blockage. The Muslim secularist's aim of keeping the door open for modernizing influences while at the same time upholding the traditional heritage represented a sort of synthesis in this polarized opposition. This role fitted the young educated Muslims perfectly:

Their primary concern was precisely to adjust to the functional requirements of modernity without getting embroiled in fundamental ideological disputes. They were able in practice to maintain this position not only because the impulse of Muslim secularism was itself profoundly ambivalent, but also because this attitude served the fundamental social interests of the newly educated Muslims of good families. This ambivalence was also manifested on a psychological level and expressed itself in a variety of ways. On the level of individual experience, for example, the educated Muslim, despite all his enthusiasm for Europe, never felt quite at home among Europeans; no matter how westernized, he could not overcome the sense of otherness which seemed quite easily surmountable by his fellow Christian Arab. This sense of otherness was reflected in the defensive attitude which Muslims always assumed with regard to their Islamic heritage and identity. Whether devout or nonpracticing, the Muslim in the West tended always to revert to a fundamentalist position and he returned from Europe convinced of Islam's inherent superiority. His defensive attitude always led to an offensive stance, which expressed itself in the polemics and apologetics characteristic of western-educated Muslims.

On another level, Muslim secularism developed a historical theory which attributed to the Arabs and Islam not just an important but a decisive role in Europe's cultural resurgence during the Middle Ages. Borrowing from Europe was simply an act of retrieving what had previously been given. This theory proved beneficial in two ways. In the first place it justified borrowing; in the second it salved the feeling of inferiority which Muslims felt toward Europe's obvious superiority in both culture and power.

As a group the Muslim secularists regarded themselves as the natural arbiters in matters dealing with relations with Europe. They also envisaged themselves as the spokesmen of the Awakening. They saw themselves as the best guardians of society's true interests and unconsciously identified their class's interests with those of society.

It must be clear by now that the educated Muslim elite seemed driven to play a special role in the Arab Awakening: as mediating agent accommodating Christian-led westernism to Islamic traditionalism as defended and upheld by the Muslim reformists and conservatives alike. In its inner development and in the positions which the Muslim secularist took with regard to the challenge of the West, we see traced some of the principal steps marking the process of social and intellectual change characteristic of this entire phase. It was the first Muslim generation to be squarely confronted with the problem of change and to be forced to contend with it on a social scale.

Despite their genuine attachment to their traditional background, the typical progressive Muslim intellectuals of this generation already began to lose their religious fervor and to break away from their traditional moorings. Their attitude toward Muslim dogma and ritual was, if not yet fully skeptical, at least cool and detached. For them Islam was slowly transformed from a meaningful faith to a symbol of identity and solidarity. In their hands the rationalism which their masters, the reformist *ulema,* had allowed to enter as a method gradually solidified into a firm (though never fully coordinated) mental framework. It should be noted, however, that neither then nor at any later stage did Muslim secularists, even in their most advanced positions, openly defy established custom and belief. In this respect a deep conservatism generally characterized their public attitudes.

Finally, from the standpoint of Muslim secularism as a whole, the abstract and theoretical implications of religion had little significance as a view of man and society. For example, on the ethical level they never presented the world and man's conflicts in religious terms, such as the Christian conceptions of tragedy or sin. The problem of evil seems not to have been seriously raised. The general Muslim secularist position lent itself to a particular attitude which spontaneously and without question accepted the "given." The suffering and injustice peculiar to social reality were not seen in a social context, but as abstract human "realities." Nor could Muslim secularism provide a principle whereby these realities could gain significance and be regarded in economic-political terms. From the point of view of both practice and theory the ontological vagueness (or innocence!) of Muslim secularism had far-reaching significance for its attitude toward Islam as a comprehensive world view. Nietzsche once urged his fellow Europeans to carry out an "autopsy" of Christianity in order to free Europe from its clutches. Such an autopsy of Islam, which only the Muslim secularists could have performed, was unthinkable.

Chapter II. Theoretical Foundations of Islamic Reformism

Basic Orientations

Islamic reformist thought was determined by its traditionalist starting points.[1] All the leading figures of the Islamic reform movement
had in common an awareness of the need to overcome the intellectual
and spiritual inertia of traditionalism,[2] but the positive aspect of this
awareness remained prescribed in both scope and relevance. Its first
step was transition from blind obedience to traditional interpretation
to a new and freer approach.[3] What this amounted to eventually was
the setting up of rational analysis (*tamhis*) as the precondition of
interpretation. This not only opened the way for the re-establishment
of the principle of independent judgment (*ijtihad*), but also questioned the authority of the established traditional hierarchy. On the
one side, this transition gave great impetus to the movement of
reform; on the other, it undermined the unity of traditional outlook.

The two most influential figures in the Islamic reform movement
were Jamal al-Din al-Afghani and Muhammad 'Abdu. Muhammad
Rashid Rida played a crucial role in disseminating their ideas (as well
as his own) through his monthly journal, *al-Manar,* which was probably the most important reformist periodical in the Muslim world for
over thirty-five years. Other important disseminators of reformist
thought were the Egyptian 'Abdallah al-Nadim (1844–96) and the
Lebanese 'Abd al-Qadir al-Mughrabi (1867–1956). The leading
spirit of Islamic reformism in Syria was Shaykh Tahir al-Jaza'iri.

It must be stressed from the start that the movement of religious
rejuvenation spearheaded by Afghani and 'Abdu did not question
doctrine. The primary impulse of reform had its source in the challenge which the West posed to Muslim society. Its aim was to protect

---

[1] We shall discuss Islamic conservatism only inasmuch as it is related to
reformism, westernism, and secularism; its position, negative and too often
empty of content, does not warrant separate treatment.

[2] Muhammad Rashid Rida, Introduction to *Tarikh al-ustadh al-imam al-
shaykh Muhammad 'Abdu* [The Life and Works of Muhammad 'Abdu] (Cairo,
1931), vol. I.

[3] "In order to reach a true understanding of a given text," Afghani declared,
"one must have intellectual freedom." Al-Mughrabi, *al-Afghani,* pp. 44–45.

Muslim society by responding to the western challenge in a "positive" way. It strove to reinstitute and strengthen Islamic truth, but not to expose it to free criticism.

Some writers have compared the movement of Islamic reform to the Protestant revolt, and 'Abdu to Luther.[4] Nothing could be further from the truth. Islamic reformism was a neo-orthodox movement, and 'Abdu's call was not for reformulation of dogma but for a return to "true" Islam. In some of its philosophical efforts this movement resembled not so much Protestantism as certain aspects of the neo-Thomist trend in twentieth-century Catholicism. But again the comparison must be taken in a narrow sense. From the doctrinal and methodological point of view, reformist thought received its inspiration primarily from the jurists and theologians of medieval Islam.[5]

It is not surprising that the attacks of the conservative *ulema* on the movement of reform never seriously questioned the doctrinal intentions of reformism. Innovation advocated by the reformists in the realm of dogma was mostly confined to formal, procedural aspects. Thus it would have been difficult for the most conservative scholar of al-Azhar, for example, to find fault in the following formulation of Islamic dogma by the leading Syrian member of the reformist *ulema* (except, perhaps, its catechistic style!):

Question: What is the meaning of Islam?
Answer: Islam is openly to declare and inwardly to believe that everything conveyed by our Prophet Muhammad is true and valid.
Question: What are the foundations of the Muslim doctrine?
Answer: The foundations of the Muslim doctrine are six: belief in God almighty, belief in his angels, belief in his Holy Book, belief in his Prophets, belief in the last judgement, and belief in Fate.[6]

[4] See 'Uthman Amin, *Ra'id al-fikr ad-misri* [The Forerunner of Egyptian Thought] (Cairo, 1955), p. 24, n.1.
[5] For example, Rida said, "What first drew my attention to . . . the necessity for reform was my reading of al-Ghazzali's treatise, *Ihya' 'ulum al-din* [The Revival of Religious Knowledge]." Cited in Shakib Arslan, *al-Sayyid Muhammad Rashid Rida aw ikha' arba'in sana* [Muhammad Rashid Rida or Forty Years' Friendship] (Damascus, 1937), p. 130.
[6] Shaykh Tahir al-Jaza'iri, *al-Jawahir al-kalamiyya fi idah al-'aqida al-islamiyya* [The Precious Words in Clarifying the Muslim Dogma] (Cairo, n.d.), p. 3. Jaza'iri, one of the least known among the leading Islamic reformists, exerted wide influence on the pre-World War I educated Muslim generation in Syria. He was responsible for liberalizing Muslim education and for founding a number of public libraries, including the famous *al-Dhahiriyya* library in Damascus. For a personal portrait by one of his more famous pupils, see Muhammad Kurd 'Ali, *Kunuz al-ajdad* [The Treasures of Ancestors] (Damascus, 1950), pp. 5–46. See also *Majalt al-majma' al-'ilmi* [Scientific Society Journal], vol. I (1921), pp. 17–21. For the only biography of Jaza'iri, see Muhammad Sa'id al-Bani, *Tanwir al-basa'ir* [Enlightenment of Minds] (Damascus, 1920). For a complete list of Jaza'iri's published and unpublished works, see Kurd 'Ali, *Kunuz*, pp. 27–28.

The reformist message was expressed not in philosophical elaborations of new ideas but mainly in two traditional forms of exposition —the religious treatise and the apologetic tract.

In its structure and style, the religious treatise is basically a modern extension of the medieval religious science of *kalam*. Yet it is different in spirit. Certainly in 'Abdu's and Jaza'iri's works one senses a certain passionate urgency beneath the placid formalism. One is aware, for instance, of a goal lying beyond the familiar positions based on traditional texts. One is conscious of a groping for a new synthesis. It is in this effort that reformist thought achieved its highest feats and exerted its greatest influence.

The apologetic part of reformist literature is quantitatively the larger. It was written from a defensive position which, however, always took an offensive attitude. Refusing to examine its own fundamental premises, it spent most of its efforts holding fast to its grounds. The apologetic effort was bound to lack the sobriety and sense of measure characteristic of the better theological works of the reformist *ulema*. Defiance concealed a timidity of spirit, and the mind was stifled by excessive rhetoric. It is not difficult to see that, in their role as defenders of Islam, the Islamic reformists undertook a task for which most of them were not really fit. But the *ulema* were the only official spokesmen of the faith.

The Postulates of Reformism

Afghani put the problem succinctly: Muslim society is sick and its salvation lay in Islam. "Every Muslim is sick, and his only remedy is in the Qur'an."[7] This formulation gave explicit expression to a dominant assumption in Islamic reformism. It explained with one stroke the cause of the prevailing ailment and named its cure. Subjectively, the disease manifested itself in loss of faith, objectively in political disintegration. The criteria for determining the cure put a high premium not on criticism and truth, but on power and success. To attain power and to achieve success led not only to social and political health; it also involved inner transformation. The key to this transformation was to be found in the Qur'an.

The linking of political decline to moral and religious decline gave the movement of Islamic reform the character of political renaissance as well as religious rebirth. Hence reformism asserted that, contrary to what foreigners and nonbelievers thought, the social and political

[7] Afghani, quoted in Muhammad al-Makhzumi, *Khatirat Jamal al-Din al-Afghani al-Husayni* [Thoughts of Jamal al-Din al-Afghani al-Husayni] (Beirut, 1931), p. 88.

malaise of the Muslim community had its source not in Islam itself, but in the Muslims. This shut the door to doctrinal criticism and placed the *ulema,* as official spokesmen of religion, in the position of leadership: With the faithful in the wrong, the power of the *ulema* was enhanced, and they arrogated the role of leading the movement of change.

In this way reformism focused on the essentially conservative and restorative effort of bringing back the faithful to the "straight path." This also accounts for the emphasis on the principle of *properly* understanding Islam. Islam in its essence was as valid as ever, only the Muslims' understanding of it was wrong: thus "Muslim backwardness was not caused by Islam but rather by the Muslims' ignorance of its truth."[8]

The *ulema* constituted the only group, Rifa'ah Rafi' al-Tahtawi (1801–73)[9] had declared a generation earlier, capable of transmitting the new learning to the younger generation. European knowledge was to be channeled through the *ulema* and its teaching supervised by them. For Tahtawi and his generation the contrast between Muslim decline and Europe's ascendancy lacked the menacing aspect it would later have for Afghani and his contemporaries. To Tahtawi Europe appeared as less of a threat than a promise. The admiration for European civilization dominating Tahtawi's own writings was combined with a spirit of self-confidence, for, though outdistanced, Islam was more than capable of catching up with contemporary Europe. The idea of inner corruption gnawing at the heart of the social structure would have seemed foreign to Tahtawi, who thought that by borrowing the right elements from Europe Islam's problems would be solved. By contrast, for Afghani's generation and that of his disciples the task was not merely to point the way to judicious borrowing from Europe; the *ulema*'s task was one of rescue in a situation of imminent shipwreck.

Islamic reformism saw the Muslim world engaged in a decisive struggle with Europe. Sometimes consciously, sometimes unconsciously, it sought to base its leadership on a foundation of political power. In order to cure the malady afflicting society, access to the

---

[8] *Ibid.,* p. 218.

[9] Rifa'ah Rafi' al-Tahtawi, *Manahij al-albab al-misriyyah fi mabahij al-adab al-'asriyyah* [The Paths of Egyptian Minds in the Joys of Modern Arts], 3d ed. (Cairo, 1912), p. 373. Tahtawi was among the first Arab intellectuals and probably the first member of the *ulema* to know Europe at first hand. He was sent by Mehmet Ali with the first Egyptian student mission to Paris (1826–30). His account of life and society in Paris and his translations and adaptations of many European works exerted a decisive influence on the Awakening in Egypt.

precincts of power was essential; hence, the apocalyptic warnings of impending disaster that Afghani and 'Abdu never tired of repeating. The *ulema*'s role was set against a background of political collapse: internally, the Muslim world had become fragmented and divided against itself, which sapped its strength and destroyed its will to fight. Now it was threatened by, or had already fallen prey to, European exploitation; Europe's interests in the Muslim world were best served by the perpetuation of the Muslims' disintegration and decline.

Islamic reformism saw itself acting "to end political disunity by reconstituting religious unity."[10] It based its "right" to leadership not only on pragmatic grounds but also on claims to religious legitimacy stemming directly from the "first legislator"—from Muhammad himself.[11]

The profound impact of Islamic reformism on the intellectual awakening during this period was the direct outcome of its success in establishing the grounds for its leadership. In Egypt this position was achieved in part through the support of the large and entrenched conservative hierarchy. No other single factor accounts as much for the sustained influence of Islamic reformism on Egyptian social and political life until the revolution of 1952.

However, despite its activism, reformist thought was basically anti-revolutionary in its social and political orientation. The theory of reform was firmly anchored in the belief that it could be effectively carried out with the consent and support of the established order.[12] And despite the reformists' hostility toward the khedive and the British, they shunned systematic radical opposition. They seemed to have the same instinctive horror of political upheaval as did their medieval forebears, the jurists and theologians who proscribed revolution even against "a tyrannical ruler." But there was no escaping political involvement, whatever form it might take. Hence, the reformist leaders always found themselves embroiled in political conflict; but their stand was hardly radical, only hostile or noncooperative. In the end, personalities mattered more than ideas, and reconciliations were not hard to effect.

Because of their function in society, the *ulema* could not have disassociated themselves from the established social order in Egypt or the Fertile Crescent. Even when their sympathy lay with the nationalist opposition (as in Egypt), they could not extricate themselves altogether from the established order. Thus the influence they exerted politically often proved a moderating one which worked in favor of

---

[10] Afghani, quoted in Rida, *Tarikh al-ustadh,* vol. I, p. 320.   [11] *Ibid.*
[12] See *al-Manar,* vol. I (1897), p. 42.

the status quo. It took another generation for a truly militant movement—capable of using violence as a means of political action—to
emerge within Islamic reformism.[13]

When they tried to define the relationship the Muslim countries
should have with Europe, the reformists experienced serious disagree-
ments within their ranks. Afghani tended toward a conservative
attitude and wished Muslims to turn back toward the Golden Age of
Islam and away from Europe. He advised the leaders of Muslim
countries not to squander their wealth "building large armies, or
trying to ally themselves with the great powers, or following the
westernizers." He implored them to shun Europe and "follow in the
footsteps of Muhammad's disciples and successors."[14]

'Abdu, though stressing the central concept of the Golden Age,
admitted more than Afghani ever did the need for modernizing
society (*tajdid*)—which could be carried out only by learning from
Europe. He accepted the principle of borrowing, while insisting that
secular reform (i.e., social and political reform) should go hand in
hand with religious reform (i.e., spiritual and moral reform). As
Muhammad Rashid Rida put it, "genuine reform . . . is impossible
without combining religious with social reform. . . . Those who seek
only political independence and social change can never succeed—
unless they join forces with the religious reformers."[15]

Reformist thought, whether addressing itself to political or social
issues, could never altogether free itself from the premises first articulated by Afghani in *al'Urwa al-Wuthqa*.[16] Afghani's preoccupation
with the "materialism" of the West reflected a general Muslim bias
toward science, which was regarded as responsible for the disintegration of traditional Christianity, and which was now threatening
Islam.[17]

To skirt this pitfall the Islamic reformists strove to distinguish
between "religious modernization" and "secular modernization." By
the former they meant a process to "purify Islam"; by the latter a
process concerned with external things not touching upon Islam as
such. Soon enough, however, they became aware of the impossibility

---

[13] E.g., the Muslim Brotherhood, founded by Hasan al-Banna in 1927.
[14] Rida, *Tarikh al-ustadh*, vol. I, p. 309.   [15] *Ibid.*, Introduction.
[16] The journal put out in Paris by Afghani and 'Abdu.
[17] Al-Mughrabi, who saw Afghani in Constantinople shortly before Afghani's
death in 1897, asked him this question: "If we compare our situation today
with what it was thirty years ago, don't we observe great progress?" Afghani
answered: "You see only the external side of things. The fact is that our
progress is nothing but retrogression and decline because it is based on
imitation of the European nations. . . ." *al-Afghani*, pp. 82–83.

of maintaining this fine distinction, and they chose to compromise with reality in order to maintain theoretical consistency. In the end, for many the protection of Islam seemed impossible by such a compromise, and they tended toward withdrawal from practical commitment—a position which Islamic conservatism had been advocating (by its behavior) all along.

The Method of Reformism

The basic assumptions of Islamic reformism are grounded in what psychologists call the "sub-theoretical" realm of outlook, the area of intuition and impulse; as such they could receive little direct or systematic expression.

It must also be pointed out that reformism as a coherent outlook possessed no clear epistemological consciousness. What awareness the reforming *ulema* had of the problem of knowledge they articulated in a most imprecise manner.

How did Islamic reformism define "reason"? What did the "rational" consist in? "Scientific reason" was the equivalent of "science," and science was defined as the power that applied itself to the material world in order to control it. As such science was anchored in fact and had little to do with truth. Truth belonged to a different order of knowledge; it had revelation as its foundation. Reason in this higher realm was illuminated by categories quite different from those peculiar to science. Reason's most immediate form was seen in the exercise of rational judgment, which distinguished the true from the false, the right from the wrong. Applied to religious and legal matters the highest form of reasoning constituted *ijtihad* (independent judgment). The reformists set great store by the "reopening of the door of *ijtihad*" and regarded it as a major starting point of the movement of religious reconstruction. The fact that, as far as concrete experience was concerned, independent reasoning provided no unifying principle for the understanding did not appear as a problem.

In its analysis Islamic reformism adhered to the traditional method of linguistic explication.[18] What is "reasonable" (*ma'qul*) was determined not in terms of an objective, empirical frame of reference but rather in terms of linguistic meaning. Admittedly there was a good deal of consistency in the steadfastness with which the Islamic reformists clung to this position, but the consistency was mostly restricted to an abstract psychological sphere. This made it much easier to deal with the threat of "scientific rationalism" and its materialistic

---

[18] I.e., "To distinguish between texts . . . and to analyze these in terms of grammar and the rules of style." *Ibid.*

presuppositions from the protected standpoint of an absolutist frame of reference. It is exactly this position which Afghani took in his principal work, *al-Radd 'ala al-dahriyyin* [The Refutation of the Materialists], which became the model for reformist thought in dealing with materialist philosophy.[19] It is not surprising if this position blocked logical discourse and contributed to deflecting interest in serious criticism.

It should be added that the attitude of mind deriving from this position was not one of conscious dishonesty on the part of individual reformists, who after all had to bear the brunt of highly sophisticated attacks on Islam. The reformist *ulema* believed that so long as they held fast to their premises and their absolutist perspective they could protect what to them was "by nature and tradition holy."[20] They knew full well that once the validity of a "scientific" starting point was granted there was no recourse from the corrosive impact of successive doubt.

One cannot escape the impression that reform was not an end in itself but rather a means to attain an end. Preoccupation of reformist thought with the threat of Europe brought about a preoccupation with power and with justification for the acquisition of power. Is it possible to understand the problem of justification without taking into account the challenge posed by Europe?

Islam, in its historical development, repeatedly experienced movements of revival and reform and underwent frequent internal changes without reference to external models. In all such instances the response to inner need had been formulated in terms of an internal frame of reference.[21]

It is quite possible that Islamic reformism might have confined itself to a *salafiyya* doctrine and become just another movement of internal "purification"—except for the threat of Europe. The distinctive achievement of Islamic reformism, which distinguishes it from all previous internal reform movements in Islam, consisted precisely in its awareness of and reaction to an external cultural and political danger. Islamic reformism regarded the attitude of the conservative

---

[19] Translated from the Persian by 'Abdu, 2d ed. (Cairo, 1955).

[20] "Cling to everything which to you is by nature and tradition holy, as a son of the Godlike West, a son of civilization." Settembrini to Hans Castrop; Thomas Mann, *The Magic Mountain* (New York, 1958), p. 243.

[21] The *sufi tariqas* (mystic brotherhoods) represent an important example. Puritanical movements, such as the Wahhabi movement (eighteenth and nineteenth centuries) in Arabia and the Mahdiyya movement (late nineteenth century) in Sudan are other examples of reform within a traditional framework.

traditionalists, who wished to close their eyes to the European challenge, not only as a negative and self-defeating attitude, but as fraught with danger to the very existence of Islamic society. Just as the conception of pan-Islamism had its roots in conservative reaction to the liberal reforms of the Ottoman Empire under the Powers' influence, the ideology of Islamic reformism received its formative impetus as a reaction to the political and intellectual challenge presented by European civilization. In this light both pan-Islamism and Islamic reformism appear as functions of the confrontation between Islam and the West in the nineteenth century.

In their most consistent position, the reformists assumed an attitude aimed at completely shutting out European influences. This, at least, was Afghani's position in his angry moments. But it was also an attitude which reformism could ill afford as a permanent policy. Compromise was not a matter of choice but an inescapable necessity. In this we see the major cause for reformism's tactical submission before pragmatic exigencies and its need for justifying retreat.

Thus it should not be surprising if the reformist *ulema* often found themselves forced to take positions which obviously did not tally with their basic theoretical premises. Thus in extreme situations the concept of reform became merely an instrument for covering up a flagrant breach of theory. In this respect reformist theory became a tool for defending Islam at any cost.

If justification was possible on the grounds of social utility, was it not possible for social utility to be made into a principle of reform? Indeed, to the reformists, this was not only logical but was indispensable for their ideology. Afghani formulated the principle succinctly: "Neither the individual nor the nation . . . nor scientific knowledge have any value except in their use."[22]

In adopting a utilitarian approach, reformist thought had to face the relativistic consequences. The *ulema* spared no effort in trying somehow to reconcile theory to practice, but in the end they had to succumb to the inherent contradiction and devise two separate levels of thought, one dealing with workaday practice and one with doctrine and dogma. As we shall see, in the hands of the secularists of educated Muslims this double standard served as an effective weapon in working loose from the clutches of traditionalism and for rational-

[22] Makhzumi, *Khatirat*, pp. 153–54. The same idea had been expressed by the Tunisian reformist Khayr al-Din, "Interest is determined by the time and the particular situation." *Muqdamat kitab aqwam al-masalik fi ma'rifat ahwal al-mamalik* (Constantinople, 1876), p. 3.

izing innovation. But in the hands of the reformist *ulema* it remained primarily a defensive weapon.

Reformist thought found itself tending toward a deterministic position, which strongly influenced its practical and theoretical attitudes. This determinism, however, was not the product of any intellectual elaboration; rather, it consisted of a dogmatic orientation expressing a deep undercurrent of fatalism.[23]

It may be said that fatalism was a mental habit of long standing in the *ulema*'s ranks. It manifested itself in two ways, one philosophical and the other psychological. Philosophically this fatalistic attitude had something Hobbesian about it: liberty and necessity are consistent; all acts are rooted in a form of necessity; although will is confined to a framework of necessity, man is nevertheless accountable for his actions. Psychologically, it assumed a different form. As the above quotation from Afghani suggests, the real problem was not philosophical—a matter of how to determine rationally the extent of man's freedom of will; it had to do with man's life and all reality, which are subject to an inexorable destiny which one could not alter and to which one could only submit. Submission was therefore not only a product of faith but an ethical principle.[24]

In confronting social reality, reformist thought was predisposed to accept as final the status quo, the form in which concrete reality presented itself. From an epistemological standpoint, what *is* held absolute primacy. Hence it was out of the question for reformists to think in terms of radical change or to proceed in terms of a revolutionary juxtaposition of elements within social reality. From this perspective it was difficult to conceive of actuality in other than casual terms or to comprehend development except chronologically. The contingent could be seen only in its ephemeral aspect, as somehow not altogether real. And insofar as action was concerned, man's power to change the world was inherently limited. Quietism presented itself as a natural political attitude. Thus from the standpoint of both understanding and action, it was simply impossible for Islamic reform-

---

[23] Afghani made a distinction between fate and determinism and considered belief in fate as a virtue: "Belief in fate, if one dissociates it from the idea of determinism, bestows on one the virtues of bravery and dauntlessness, of manly courage and heroism; it brings to one resolution that will enable him to face supreme danger. . . ." *al-'Urwa*, vol. I (1884); see Rida, *Tarikh al-ustadh*, vol. I, p. 325.

[24] E.g., "Ra's al-hikma makhafat al-llah" [The essence of wisdom is fear of God].

ism to elaborate a theory of reform that could in the least bit be revolutionary.

In certain of its moments and despite its apparent practicality, reformist thought was prey to much self-questioning, even despair. The following quotations will give an idea of two different aspects of this peculiar *état d'esprit*.

> We[25] were at the home of the Imam ['Abdu] talking about what we had just heard, namely, that the Japanese wished to adopt Islam. Shaykh Husayn al-Jisr exclaimed: "Islam now has hope to regain its former power and glory."
>
> [Shaykh Salman, d. 1918] answered: "Leave [the Japanese] alone. If they are converted to Islam we will probably corrupt them before they ever have the chance to reform us. . . . We will yet see the result of the hopes you put in this moribund [Muslim] nation and of the reforms you attempt to carry out in this decayed [Arab] society . . ."

The other reflects a different and more profound despair.[26]

> If we are true Muslims in the full sense of the word . . . why is it then that God has not kept his promise to us? In the Qur'an He promised the faithful and the doers of good works that they will achieve success on this earth. . . . Why has He not bestowed success on us but has instead given it to others who are not of the Faith? Why is it that we are everywhere defeated and subjugated by our enemies?

This sense of frustration exerted a profound influence on the development of reformist thought, particularly in political matters, which probably explains its excessive emphasis on power and material strength. Thus, owing to Islam's obvious material and military inferiority, reformism's pride expressed itself defensively, but this defensiveness took on an aggressive form—the better to conceal its tormenting sense of helplessness. It was only natural that a state of mind such as this should tend to seek protection by barricading itself in the vision of a glorious past.

In this light it is impossible to interpret Islamic reformism purely in terms of its discursive rational formulations. It is necessary to turn, as we shall in Chapter III, to the emotional wells which provided the fundamental impulses of its ideology.

Hasan Rida, a contemporary Egyptian writer, has written deri-

---

[25] A number of 'Abdu's disciples, gathered in 'Abdu's house shortly after the news of Japan's victory over Russia in 1905; the conversation is reported by Rida. See Louis Cheikho, *al-Adab al-'arabiyya fi al-rub' al-awwal min al-qarn al-ishrin* [Arabic Literature in the First Quarter of the Twentieth Century] (Beirut, 1926), p. 94.

[26] 'Abd al-Qadir al-Mughrabi, *al-Bayyinat* [Collected Essays] (Cairo, A. H. 1344), vol. I, pp. 5–6.

sively of the sterility and shallowness of the Islamic reformists' analysis of the social problem.[27] Indeed, he is correct in saying that there was an air of "grammatical preoccupation" about the way in which Islamic reformists generally handled the burning issues of the day. But given its starting points, the reformists' position could not have been otherwise.

Reformist thought was, from a methodological standpoint, too ill-equipped to achieve a rational and focused consciousness of social reality. It lacked the basic precondition for such consciousness—the capacity for self-corrective criticism. From the perspective of the present, it is easy to see the failings of this outlook. The fact remains that the reformists, though prey to recurrent failure of nerve, never really engaged in systematic rational doubt. Despite much confusion and despair they managed to stand their ground.

When one reads Afghani and 'Abdu in their short-lived biweekly *al-'Urwa al-Wuthqa* (or in Rida's Cairo-based *al-Manar*), one cannot but be impressed by the toughness of their reforming zeal. There is not the slightest hint of admitting a contrary or alternative position; at the same time, there is no possibility for self-examination or for turning the eye inward. The discussions always revolved around questions that one knew in advance could be resolved. At the height of their productive period they lived and wrote amid clamor; there was not much time for reflection, not much time for silence. Reality in these writings appears as a table of fixed, absolute ideas. Far from stooping to examine its tools, their thought leans back on pre-established universal certainties.

The Goals of Reformism

Islamic reformism's two main goals—the restoration of Islam's hegemony and its precondition—the revival of true religion—were to be achieved through interrelated means. The task of reviving the true Islam had logical as well as practical primacy and required substantive changes in the traditional approach to doctrinal interpretation and analysis. Afghani, in his talks and lectures, formulated the general direction Islamic revival was to take; but it was 'Abdu who, using Afghani's teachings as a springboard, gave this direction its precise formulation. 'Abdu delineated four main stages for the process of revival.

The first stage was, in 'Abdu's words, to "liberate the mind from

---

[27] "Les discussions sur le système social prennent l'aspect de controverses grammaticales." Hasan Rida, *L'Égypte nassérienne* (Paris, 1964), p. 235.

the bonds of 'imitative reasoning.' "[28] Thus from the start the problem was set against the background of the traditionalist outlook. Here 'Abdu laid the foundation for subsequent reformist effort in dealing with the conservative approach to Islamic dogma.

The second stage was attainment of the "proper understanding" of religion. Emphasis was again put on approach rather than doctrine. By focusing on the period of Muhammad and his immediate successors, the Orthodox Caliphs (522–662), 'Abdu sought (and in this was directly inspired by Afghani) to evoke a vision of a Golden Age of Islam. Then Islam was uncomplicated by the elaborations and constructions of the jurists and theologians of later times. In pursuing this line of thought 'Abdu evaded direct confrontation with the schools (*madhahib*) of orthodox Islam. He was always mindful of the fact that controversy would only arouse further disunity and thus increase Muslim weakness. Moreover, by turning to the model of early Islam there were other gains to be made. True knowledge derived from the original source led directly to virtue and to strength. By adhering to the word of God as conveyed to Muhammad in the Qur'an and by following Muhammad's example, Muslims would find the source of true Islam and therein the basis of indissoluble unity.

This led to the definition of the third stage, which became a cardinal reformist tenet: Final authority in all that concerned religious doctrine lay neither in the schools nor in the religious heirarchy, but in the Qur'an and the *Sunna* (Muhammad's sayings and practice). With one stroke he divested conservative traditionalism of its sharpest weapon and challenged it on its own grounds. Here lies the primary cause for the conservatives' bitter hostility toward the movement of reform: the conservative *ulema* owed their position and power to the very system which reformism now wished to change. 'Abdu's seemingly harmless call to "return to the original springs of Islam" constituted a direct threat to the established clerical hierarchy, because his demand, carried to its logical conclusion, would have produced radical changes in the institutional structure of Islam. But this did not happen. By positing final authority for legitimation in the Qur'an and Muhammad's *Sunna,* the reformist *ulema* only gained a strategically advantageous position. In a sense, they succeeded in wiping the slate clean; they could interpret the Law anew, in the light of the peculiar requirements of the time. It was as though 'Abdu wanted to blot out twelve centuries of unsatisfactory history and

---

[28] I.e., *taqlid*. "Imitative reasoning" in its proper context is the opposite of "independent reasoning" (*ijtihad*).

make a fresh start. He apparently believed that all the mistakes and misfortunes of the intervening centuries were the result of some sort of misunderstanding.

The fourth stage was the establishment of rational criteria of interpretation—"of considering religious truth rationally." At first sight this may appear to be 'Abdu's most original contribution to the reformist movement. But was it not in fact *ijtihad* that 'Abdu was now again talking about? From his own formulations it is difficult to make the distinction. True, there seems to be a new spirit, a deep sense of urgency, in the way he dealt with certain "rational" problems. He seemed, particularly in the early writings, on the verge of breaking through to a new conception of what reform ought to be. But he always curbed his ideas and never allowed himself to overstep the conventional limits. In the end one is left with the impression that what he really meant by "human reason" was simply the need for logical discourse. With time, his pressing concern, as well as that of his disciples, tended to center more and more on simply breaking the hold of the stereotypes of "imitative reasoning" (*taqlid*). In short, the critical consciousness which a genuine rationalism would have necessarily required failed to emerge.

It must be noted, however, that the introduction of the idea of rational reasoning did effect some gain for reformism. In the first place it bestowed greater maneuverability on reformist thought. It made it easier to cope with de facto and irrevocable change. By the use of "rational" terms, theory could be adjusted to practice with less pain and inconvenience. In this, "rationalism" as a principle of interpretation provided the requisite psychological resilience which was altogether absent in the stereotyped categories of conservative thought.

The principle of rationality also served to advance a modicum of change. The actual pattern of borrowing was rendered more systematic by the possibility of rationalizing it. Pragmatic necessity could no longer be effectively opposed by unthinking traditionalism. Reformist rationalism helped pave the way for explaining the need for certain reforms, particularly in the political sphere.

It must be added that, to the extent that reformist rationalism was successful in achieving its objectives, it contributed to corroding the traditional foundations from which it itself had emerged and in which it was ultimately based. Thus even though 'Abdu's rationalism may not have become a developed and fully effective critical instrument, it served as a double-edged sword.

Political Commitments

Both 'Abdu and Afghani started out as rebels; they both ended up reconciled conservatives. Afghani has been portrayed as the moving spirit of Egypt's awakening in the 1870s and the inspirer of the 'Urabi movement and of Egyptian nationalism.[29] Had he kept to his original course, one of his close collaborators wrote, "he would have brought about Egypt's political transformation."[30] As it happened, he was forced to leave the country and did not take part in the critical events that preceded the British occupation of Egypt in 1882. For the next twenty years, except for a brief period in Persia (where he felt at home[31]), he was destined to a life of exile. 'Abdu, who was a young man when the 'Urabi revolt broke out in 1881, soon discovered that by temperament and disposition he was not suited for the role of political activist.[32] For a short while he too was forced into exile. When he returned to Egypt in 1888 at the age of thirty-nine the activist phase of his life was already behind him. He settled down to a life of government service, which was crowned before his death by his appointment to the position of Grand Mufti (jurisconsult) of Egypt, the highest religious office in the land.

It was during their period of exile that Afghani and 'Abdu produced most of the ideas that made their mark on Arab political thought. Their center was Paris and their mouthpiece the biweekly *al-'Urwa al-Wuthqa.*

Paris of the Third Republic was the Mecca for political exiles from all over the Ottoman Empire and Eastern Europe. Since the early nineteenth century France had been Britain's chief European rival in the Middle East and the traditional ally of Egypt and friend of the Ottoman Empire. France was also the home of the French revolution, the center of democracy in Europe. For the political exile, Paris was not only a place of refuge, it was a spiritual home.

[29] "He was the first reformer of al-Azhar and the first to reform Muslim education. . . . He was the founder of the National Party which sought to base government on national foundations. . . . Afghani's lasting achievement was in Egypt." Rida, *Tarikh al-ustadh,* vol. I, p. 79.

[30] See Muhammad Khalaf al-Llah, *'Abdallah al-Nadim wa mudhakkiratihi al-siyasiyyah* [Abdallah Nadim and His Political Memoirs] (Cairo, 1956), p. 53.

[31] Afghani came from a Persian family, probably of the Muslim Shi'i sect. See his nephew's testimony, Lutfallah Khan, *Jamal al-Din al-Asdabadi, al-ma'ruf bil-Afghani* [Jamal al-Din al-Asdabadi. Known as al-Afghani], trans. Sadiq Nash'at and 'Abd al-Mun'im Hasanayn (Cairo, 1957).

[32] His collapse and recantation after a few months in jail in 1882 are recounted by the British lawyer appointed to defend him. For text of the report, see Rida, *Tarikh al-ustadh,* vol. I, pp. 225–33.

But for Afghani and 'Abdu, life in Paris was neither easy nor, apparently, pleasant. 'Abdu, who had first gone to Beirut after his expulsion from Egypt, joined Afghani in Paris in 1884. They lived in a small apartment near the Place de la Madeleine, where they did their cooking and worked on the journal. They faced acute economic hardships throughout their stay in Paris.

This was not a period of rewarding and cheerful achievement, as portrayed by later writers. Their life was dominated by loneliness and homesickness. They saw few people, and associated mostly with other "orientals"—Muslims from India, Persia, Egypt, and the Ottoman Empire. They hardly knew any Frenchmen. Except for occasional meetings with French orientalists and a few politicians interested in the East,[33] they were completely cut off from their Parisian environment. Their command of the French language, especially 'Abdu's, appears to have been hardly adequate.

The experience of exile exercised great influence on the direction of Afghani's and 'Abdu's thought during this crucial phase. Exile imposed its own peculiar perspective. The outside world appeared meaningful, not in terms of what was given, but in reference to another, absent world. The present was an interlude; time was the vehicle of memory and the avenue of hope. For the two reformists there was no expectation of real or immediate change in Egypt or in any part of the Ottoman Empire. Despite their passionate words, they were gradually moving toward a position of reconciliation. Estranged in the heart of Europe, they turned to a nostalgic, increasingly mystical vision of Islam; they saw in it all that European civilization had to offer and more.

Their political activity during this period went in three main directions: they drew up formal protests, which they directed to "European public opinion"; they defended Islam publicly and in private discussions; and they made feeble attempts at political conspiracy.

In their protests and in their defense of Islam they established a practice which Arab spokesmen of a later time were to follow. The premise which they unconsciously posited was that the solution of Islam's (political) problems lay in the end in the hands of Europeans. Engaging in lengthy and earnest attempts at setting forth the justice of their cause, they believed that they were effectively influencing the

[33] On one occasion Afghani met Victor Hugo, a refreshing interlude in the drabness of daily existence. Afghani is reported to have put this question to the aged poet: "Quelle est la chose que vous avez trouvée la plus admirée dans le cours de votre existence, la chose que vous avez trouvée la plus parfaite, la plus belle, la meilleure de toutes?" "C'est la rose," answered Hugo. *Orient*, no. 21 (1962), p. 207.

attitude of Europeans and the policies of the big powers. They seemed convinced that if the truth were presented forcefully enough it would automatically engender backing and support. They contributed to establishing the belief, which other Arab leaders were later to uphold, that whatever conflict of interest existed between Islam and the West, it was in the end solvable if only reason and justice were made to prevail.

Their "conspiratorial" activities were limited to "secret" talks with other exiled groups and to vague plans that never came to anything. For Afghani and 'Abdu (as for all frustrated political activists) writing and thinking and talking about political change brought with it the desire to bring about change. Afghani, failing to re-enter Egypt, succeeded in finding his way to Persia, from whence he shortly left for Turkey, where he lived in semi-isolation until his death (in 1897) from mouth cancer. As for 'Abdu, he lived a quiet but busy life in his native land. During this period he devoted himself to improving the quality of Islamic courts in Egypt and to attempting to reform the educational system of al-Azhar.

Chapter III. The Ideology of Islamic Reformism

It is in confronting an external threat or in embarking upon a course of collective action that a social group has its greatest need for ideology. The functional value of an ideology increases in proportion to stress. The more shaken the Islamic reformists' position became (and the greater the threat of Europe appeared), the more reliance they were forced to put on ideological constructions.

Inability to face facts, Mannheim has said, creates its own ideology. In the case of reformism it was not so much the inability to face facts as it was the lack of a systematic understanding of them that led to increasing dependence on ideological elaborations. The reformists were unable fully to take account of the process of change with which Islam was faced and which it tried to control. As things happened, social conduct changed first, and the ideas and norms by which it was governed changed later. Divorced from the rapidly changing reality around them, the reformists found themselves more and more in need, not of theories of interpretation, but of slogans to justify their actions. Ideas of independent reasoning and theories of interpretation seemed insufficient to crystallize a political attitude.

Reformist ideology (like all "derivations") had only indirect relation to rational grounds. It was constantly impelled to break away from religious theory in order to build political bases.[1] The ideological structure which evolved from this will to action served not only to portray social reality from a different standpoint, but to explain it in a different way. For to deal with a reality and to sustain purposeful existence, it was necessary to view it not as it actually was but in a manner that bestowed upon it desired, tolerable meaning. What reformist ideology concealed and what it attempted to accommodate revealed its hopes and anxieties and fears.

The development of reformist ideology was strongly influenced by an element inherent in the Muslim outlook. Islamic society (like the Chinese and Indian societies) lacked the idea of duality between ethics and politics. This accounts in large part for the indifference

[1] "Tout commence en mystique et finit en politique," as Charles Péguy put it,

with which the reformists accepted contradictions in their thought. It also explains the facile utilitarianism with which they tackled certain problems.

An important aspect of the development of reformist ideology lay in the fact that it did not confine itself to doctrinal grounds but drew on sources other than its own. From this broadened base it was able to appeal successfully to Islamic conservatives with regard to certain issues and to Christian modernists and Muslim secularists on others. This ideology dominated the consciousness of the age until just before the outbreak of World War I.

Reformist thought often stressed values and goals which, if pushed to their limit, would have subverted its fundamental premises. My concern here, however, is not with analyzing theoretical validity or consistency, but with explaining intent. Whatever the source or structure of meaning in reformist ideology, its interest for this study lies in the psycho-sociological purpose it served. In a sense, it was nothing more than a "definition of the situation"[2]—as it was and as it ought to be. This "definition" is precisely what gave reformist ideology its significance.

In the following pages we shall describe the definitions reformism gave to its social-historical situation and outline the principal motifs which to this day characterize the "Islamic position" in Arab political life.

Rationalization of Decline

Wherein lay the cause of Islamic decline? If Islam itself was the cause, then obviously there was no hope for salvation. But from the standpoint of Islamic reformism, "corruption never touched Islam"[3] —a cardinal ideological starting point elaborated by every leading reformist. For both conservatives and reformists this conception was irrefutable. But whereas conservatism could afford to close its eyes to the problem of Islamic decline, reformism had to rationalize it.

Decline was neither providential nor accidental. It was the result of historical events which go as far back as the first Muslim century, when disagreement and civil war led to the collapse of Islamic unity. The Golden Age ended quite early in Muslim history according to reformist ideology. The virtue of this line of thought lay not only in providing a convenient explanation but it also suggested a solution.

Before Islam, the Arabs were an obscure and insignificant collec-

[2] In the sense used by Karl Mannheim, *Ideology and Utopia* (New York, n.d.), pp. 21–22.
[3] For Afghani's theory of "religious reform," see al-Mughrabi, *al-Bayyinat,* vol. I, pp. 3–4.

tion of warring tribes. It was Islam which brought them unity and power, delivered them from barbarism, and gave them a great civilization. From the present state of disunity and decline there was no deliverance except by restoring that phase of Islam. Not only would the Arabs restore their political power, but they would also revive their great civilization.

Ironically, a good part of the reformists' ideological ammunition came from the West, from the works of European historians and orientalists. The image of early Islam was greatly expanded by the European scholars whom the reformists took as witnesses and supporters of their cause. Nothing could have been more satisfying than having Europeans acknowledge Islam's great contribution. Europe's verdict became an ideological banner around which reformism rallied its forces.

As might be expected, the translations made from European works were the ones most complimentary to Islam. Many scholarly works were ignored in favor of the flattering and more flamboyant ones. It was perhaps inevitable that the romantic and sentimental spirit with which some European authors dealt with Muslim culture was absorbed into reformist ideology. The self-image which Islamic ideology propagated in the Arab and Muslim worlds was greatly affected by these conceptions.

The idealization of Islam served to combat the feeling of inferiority. The Islamic renaissance was portrayed as opening a new and glorious chapter in the history of the Islamic people. A restored Islam was more than capable of facing up to Europe. Even in terms of power it could meet Europe on an equal footing. After all, had not the Muslim nation been "one of the greatest military nations in history?"[4]

Yet the success of resurgent Islam was to be achieved by nothing other than its intrinsic, universal truth. Europeans, Americans, and Asians would be made to understand the great message which Muhammad had brought, and they would be induced to adopt it. Among the western nations, Americans seemed the most apt to adopt Islam, for "between them and the Muslims there [was] not the same hostility and mistrust which existed between Muslims and Europeans."[5] But even the Europeans could be won over eventually. "We can attract them to us and make them trust us," said Afghani.[6] The Japanese, a

---

[4] Rida, *Tarikh al-ustadh*, vol. I, p. 325.
[5] Al-Mughrabi, *al-Afghani*, p. 57.
[6] He suggested accomplishing this by proving to Europeans that "we ourselves are not good Muslims . . ." so as not to judge true Islam by the condition of contemporary Muslims. Al-Mughrabi, *al-Bayyinat*, vol. I, p. 10.

"sister Eastern nation," were the people most prepared to accept Islam. At the time of Japan's victory over Russia, Islam, it was rumored, was quickly spreading in Japan.[7]

Superiority of the West

There was another stubborn fact: how to account for Europe's superiority? Islamic conservatism was consistent in insisting on Islam's self-sufficiency and in opposing all forms of borrowing western ideas and institutions. Reformism, on the other hand, could not deny the facts: Europe's presence was overpowering, and her military and industrial superiority could not be denied. The sense of self-preservation demanded that this challenge be faced squarely. Reformism once more took the offensive in order to defend Islam.

Europe's inherent superiority was denied in the same way that Islam's inherent inferiority had been proven wrong. In the first place, there were no racial or ethnic grounds for the Europeans' superiority.[8] Muslims as well as all other non-Europeans could attain the same level of civilization and progress.[9] Muslims lacked only one element which if possessed could transform the entire relationship between Islam and the West. This element was 'ilm, scientific knowledge. By scientific knowledge the reformists did not mean a mental attitude or technique, but rather a secret that automatically bestowed power on its possessor. Hence Afghani's often quoted assertion: "The very existence of the East depends on acquiring scientific knowledge; it is the instrument with which it can crush the power of the West . . . and its people achieve their liberation."[10]

This position, at least the main ideas supporting it, was held by the two leading intellectuals of the previous generation who had first-hand knowledge of European civilization, Rifa'ah Rafa' al-Tahtawi and Khayr al-Din Pasha (d. 1889). They both had developed a thesis which now became central in reformist ideology: that Europe's civilization (and therefore its scientific knowledge) was based largely on what Europe had borrowed from Islam. Tahtawi said that Euro-

---

[7] See p. 33, above.

[8] 'Abdallah al-Nadim, *Sulafat 'Abdallah al-Nadim* [Best Writings of 'Abdallah al-Nadim], ed. 'Abd al-Fattah al-Nadim (Cairo, 1901–14), vol. II, pp. 109–20.

[9] In an article published in 1892 al-Nadim wrote derisively of western claims that nonwestern nations "could have no existence except through the West, achieve no glory except through association with the West, and gain no honor except by being able to speak the languages of the West . . ." and mocked its claim to being "the source of law, the home of science and virtue. . . ." *Ibid.*, p. 65.

[10] Makhzumi, *Khatirat*, p. 142.

pean knowledge "only seems foreign [to Muslims]; it is in origin Islamic."[11] He maintained that, in any case, most of it had been "translated from Arabic."[12]

Khayr al-Din, a practical man motivated by political considerations as well as by ideological interests, had gone even further. He was certain that Europe would extend its domination over the Arab world unless the Arabs took "the right steps to reform their political institutions."[13] The only way this could be done, he said, was by borrowing the ideas and institutions of Europe. He backed his recommendation by two arguments: first, that "Muslim law does not prohibit reforms designed to strengthen economic and cultural life";[14] and second, that "since European civilization was based mostly on what Islam had contributed to it in the past, it was the duty [of Muslims] to take it back."[15]

Thus, just as true understanding of Islam had shown Islam to be both incorruptible and inviolable, true understanding of Europe revealed the extent to which Europe was indebted to Islam. The reformists now said that even the most recent revolutionary theories in science had their origins in Muslim contributions. For example, Darwin had long been anticipated by Muslim scientists. "The theory of evolution . . . was known to the Arabs long before Darwin—we must, however, acknowledge the man's perseverance."[16] Even 'Abdu resorted to the same formula: "We only take back what we had originally given."[17] But 'Abdu also stressed the intrinsic elements of European civilization.

Now that this argument was expressed in quasireligious terms, reformist ideology made a profound impression on the younger Muslim generation. Later it was incorporated into nationalist ideology, and it even made an impact on Christian westernizing thought. Jurji Zaydan (d. 1914), the sober editor of *al-Hilal* and one of the leading Christian intellectuals of this period, maintained that many of Europe's cultural acquisitions were originally derived from the Arabs. Europe enriched these acquisitions by new discoveries and inventions.[18] This trend of thought was given added impetus by generalizations made by arabophile European historians.

---

[11] Tahtawi, *Manahij*, p. 373. In another work written in the 1830s he described it as "the knowledge which had been lost" by the Muslims and which should be repossessed. *Taklis al-ibriz ila talkis Bariz* [Customs and Manners of the Modern French] (Cairo, 1905), p. 79.

[12] Tahtawi, *Manahij*, p. 373.   [13] Masalik, p. 64.   [14] *Ibid.*, p. 63.

[15] *Ibid.*, p. 6.   [16] Makhzumi, *Khatirat*, pp. 183, 186.

[17] "Comments on a Mistake made by Reasonable People," *al-Manar*, vol. IX (1906), pp. 597–98.

[18] Rida, *Tarikh al-ustadh*, vol. IV, p. 165.

The Relationships of Power

It is important to keep in mind that reformist ideology was formed during the height of European imperialism. In 1877 Turkey was attacked by Russia; in 1881 Tunisia was occupied by France; and in 1882 Egypt was occupied by Great Britain. By 1914 Libya, Morocco, and most of Turkey's possessions in Europe had fallen under European domination.[19] More and more Europe was being viewed in terms of imperialism and less and less in terms of its cultural attributes.

A negative, hostile attitude thus crystallized toward Europe in the last decade or two of the nineteenth century. In Tahtawi and Khayr al-Din there had been, as we have seen, a kind of relaxed detachment toward Europe. Though they were concerned with the European threat as a theoretical problem, their main interest was to determine the criteria to be employed in borrowing from Europe—in exploiting European knowledge. They were confident that the Muslim world was able to keep Europe at bay. Tahtawi had come to manhood when Egypt under Muhammad Ali was a Mediterranean power. He and his generation viewed the European states from a position of power. Khayr al-Din, though keenly aware of Europe's superiority, was confident that the Ottoman Empire would maintain its place among the great powers. For them the only thing necessary was to reform the "secular institutions." Indeed, they were certain that not only was the Muslim world capable of dealing with Europe; it would sooner or later catch up with it.

Reformist ideology reflected the changed circumstances of the later part of the nineteenth century. Pessimism regarding the future fed on increasing suspicion and fear of European imperialism. Westernization became suspect because it brought domination closer. Every gesture by a European power became the object of mistrust; every kindly act concealed an ulterior motive. In all their efforts the European powers were seen to be motivated by predatory ambitions; they offered help only in order to colonize. Indeed, the means of domination were seldom those of direct conquest. "No European power ever entered an Eastern country as a self-professed conqueror; it always established itself under the guise of reform, in the name of civiliza-

---

[19] In the late 1870s Adib Ishaq (1856–85), the Syrian Christian writer living in Egypt, had speculated: "If Russia attacked eastern Asia Minor, Austria Turkey's Balkan possessions, Britain Egypt and the islands of the Eastern Mediterranean, France the Phoenician coast and Syria, Italy Tunisia and the adjacent territories, and Spain Morocco—what will be left of us . . .?" 'Abboud, *Ruwwad,* p. 192.

tion."[20] Imperialism more often than not achieved its objectives gradually, through financial and economic means.[21]

A fundamental tenet of reformist ideology evolved from a growing awareness of Europe's imperialistic ambitions. In this light, Europe could have nothing to offer Islam that was not tainted by its rapacious intentions toward the Islamic countries. Islam could not wish to borrow from it anything except those elements which directly led to acquiring the means of defending itself, to the possession of power. On the highest plane, these means again presented themselves in terms of *'ilm;* more directly, they consisted of new weapons and military organization and technique. Europe was now seen not so much as the seat of civilization, but as a civilization that possessed the secret of power and domination.

Islamic Solidarity

It was reformist ideology that first formulated the threat posed by imperialism in terms of the confrontation between Islam and Christendom. The memory of the crusades was invoked and Muslims were now called upon to rally to the defense of the faith. The concept of holy war (*al-jihad al-muqaddas*) was revived, and defiance to the West received definite content by explicit analogy. Here reformist ideology elaborated its most potent antiwestern slogans, appealing to both the educated elite and the illiterate masses. Probably no other single ideological formulation (until the rise of the revolutionary left in the 1960s) has had as strong an effect on Arab political consciousness as this call to defiance.

It was only natural that the appeal to Islamic solidarity should find its firmest grounds in the concept of pan-Islamism. But the reformist idea of pan-Islamism is not to be confused with Abdul Hamid's policy —though in ideological terms there was no opposition between the two positions. Indeed, the Islamic reformists gave their full support to Abdul Hamid's efforts to pursue a pan-Islamic course. But it was clear that while the latter's motivation was fundamentally determined by Ottoman interests, reformist pan-Islamism was grounded in doc-

---

[20] Al-Nadim, *Sulafat,* vol. II, p. 69.

[21] Describing Europe's economic imperialism, al-Nadim wrote: "Europe declares: 'You are primitive peoples because you do not know how to make your clothing or manufacture your furniture. You need our products. But you will not be able to get them until you sign commercial agreements with us.' This way Europe was able to flood the countries of Asia and Africa with its goods and to take away their wealth. . . . Thus the people of the East have become reduced to the status of coolies—to sow, farm and labor in order to be able to purchase Europe's products and increase Europe's wealth . . . as if they were created from a different mold to serve Europeans." *Ibid.,* p. 65.

trinal considerations embracing the entire Muslim *ummah* (community). This impulse to unite is at the source of all later unitary conceptions. It required but one step to move from the idea of pan-Islamism to that of pan-Arabism.

Islamic reformist ideology, so long as it maintained its ascendency, would accept no ideological formulation of the situation other than its own, and least of all a nationalist (i.e., secular) formulation. It directed its particular antagonism toward western-inspired nationalism, which tended to underrate the religious element of solidarity in favor of culture, history, and language. It is not surprising that those who spoke in nationalistic terms were accused by the reformists of serving the interests of imperialism—a practice which the nationalists later adopted to attack their own adversaries. This accusation also fell on Christian intellectuals, who, as advocates of modernization, naturally upheld secular conceptions of society and state derived from European models. But reformist hostility was mostly directed against the young educated Muslims who increasingly tended toward the idea of nationhood.

The reformist attitude toward the emerging nationalist ideology remained uncompromisingly hostile to the end, insisting that the religious bond, not the bond of nationality, constituted the foundation of unity. This is why the reformist *ulema* considered it essential always to emphasize not Arab brotherhood, but the brotherhood of Muslims—"the Turk, the Arab, the Persian, the Egyptian, the Maghribi, and the Indian Muslim."[22] "Muslims," declared Afghani, "form one nation because they belong to one Faith."[23]

Political and Social Ideology

Surprisingly, reformist thought made little use of history as an instrument of ideology. It presented history not as an intelligible, comprehensive scheme, but rather as a formless flow. It did not attribute special significance to historical unfolding, nor did it see it in terms of a particular purpose or end. The idea of evolution was generally only obscurely perceived, and its significance for a historical vision of reality was never fully appreciated. Probably sensing evolution's adverse philosophical implications for religious dogma, the reformists kept away from it.

Reformism could neither free itself from the weight of traditional dogmatism nor properly adapt itself to the new "modern" concepts. It seemed utterly unable, above all in its social and political formula-

---

[22] Rida, *Tarikh al-ustadh*, vol. I, p. 324.   [23] *Ibid.*, vol. I, p. 328.

tions, to make the needed distinction between the temporal and religious spheres of action. Overcome by the onrush of new ideas, reformism was obliged constantly to justify, rationalize, and retreat. With their backs to the wall, the reformist writers were finally driven to a sort of de facto surrender, which is best seen in the impotent affirmation that the political and social values of Islam are identical with those of modern Europe.[24]

What were some of the distinctive features of reformism which brought it to this impasse?

Gradualism. Reformist ideology insisted on the evolutionary (as opposed to the revolutionary) approach for carrying out social change.[25] Most reformists feared violence and distrusted political radicalism of any kind. They could not believe that anything positive could result from disrupting the social order. The Islamic reformists were never able to work out—as did certain westernizing Christian intellectuals, for example—effective categories for the understanding of political action and motivation. Reformist thought remained blind to the goals of radical thought.

The reformist writers justified their predilection for the nonrevolutionary approach on theoretical as well as practical grounds. Thus one argument was that it is against the natural order of things to force change: "Reform in all its forms must be introduced step by step in accordance with the laws of nature."[26] From the practical point of view, if change was to be lasting, it had to be carried out slowly; for "what is hastily erected collapses rapidly and reverts to its original state."[27]

Legitimacy. Reformist ideology insisted that there was a qualitative difference between European and Muslim authority owing to the grounds from which each derived its legitimacy. The former applied solely to the temporal sphere, in which man was viewed from the standpoint of his empirical existence; the latter did not distinguish between the temporal and the spiritual.[28] Thus obedience to authority

[24] See Albert Hourani, *Arabic Thought in the Liberal Age,* 1798–1939 (London, 1962), pp. 191–92.

[25] 'Abdu's advice was to emphasize education and to seek governmental aid. "We must concentrate on education; we must urge the government to be just and fair; we must make attractive the idea of local and district advisory councils." Rida, *Tarikh al-ustadh,* vol. I, p. 217.

[26] Jaza'iri in al-Bani, *Tanwir,* p. 79.   [27] *Ibid.*

[28] Rida put it as follows: "Whereas foreign [i.e., European] governments . . . have sovereignty over men's bodies, which is exercised by means of coercion, Muslim rulers have two kinds of power over their subjects, physical power . . . and spiritual authority, which exerts moral pressure." *al-Manar,* vol. IX (1906), p. 418.

could not be merely the result of socially enacted law but the product of religious and moral obligations. Violation of this principle either by the ruler or the ruled inevitably led to political disintegration.

There is perhaps a faint echo of "social contract" in this position since the right of subjects to disobey their sovereign is implicitly suggested. Nevertheless political opposition is far from encouraged or even justified, for the subjects could withhold obedience not because of contractual breach on the ruler's part, but because of some transcendental principle. In short, it was not the subject's rights that were emphasized, but the grounds legitimizing the ruler's power. Thus reformist ideology in effect inhibited the idea of popular sovereignty by investing political authority with extralegal, transcendental legitimacy. And although it paid lip service to constitutional government and representative democracy, it nevertheless upheld the principles supporting theocratic rule and monarchial absolutism.

Democracy and socialism. Indeed, the source of Islamic reformism's deepest anxiety was precisely in connection with the westernizing theories favoring adoption of European political forms and institutions. The reformist authors insisted on Islam's intrinsic capacity for modernity, and on the essential "congruence between Islam and modernity."[29] Democracy as a principle of political organization was shown to have deep roots in the practice of the early Muslim community. There was no point in turning to Europe when Muslims could find their best guide in their own heritage. What Islamic democracy in the Golden Age had to offer was far superior to anything provided by Europe.

The doctrine of socialism was rejected on similar grounds. As it arose in Europe it was seen as based on nothing but hatred and oppression.[30] No European political thinker was ever able to come forth with a socialist doctrine that could be "rationally acceptable."[31] True socialism, like genuine democracy, was to be found in Islam.[32]

Islamic reformist ideology sought in this way to combat Europe not merely by showing the inadequacy of its political ideas and institutions but by proving that Islam possessed better ideas and better institutions. It sought to repel Europe's ideological aggression by employing European ideas clothed in Islamic garb. But its real prob-

---

[29] This was also stated in a generalized manner: ". . . there is no opposition between science and religion, as pointed out by the philosopher Spencer and other materialist philosophers." al-Bani, *Tanwir*, pp. 47–48.

[30] Makhzumi, *Khatirat*, p. 190.

[31] Rida, *al-Manar*, vol. I (1897), p. 946.

[32] Makhzumi, *Khatirat*, p. 194; Rida rejected Bolshevism in terms of Islamic values, *al-Manar*, vol. XXIII (1920), p. 254.

lem lay in the fact that Europe's ideologies were championed not only by Christians but also by Muslims. This is why the reformists launched their fiercest attacks against those intellectuals who called for secularism in political life (e.g., the separation of church and state) as the precondition for social reform.[33] Reformist ideology put forth the claim that, without achieving intellectual independence from Europe and setting up the Islamic intellectual tradition as its source of inspiration, true reform would be impossible.

The *ulema* soon recognized that the young western-educated Muslims constituted the really serious threat to all they stood for. The Christian westernizing intellectuals posed a different kind of threat: they were the native conveyors of Europe's culture who performed the same task as their missionary coreligionists. But when it came to the new type of educated Muslim, "who no longer seriously cared for religion . . . who neither prayed nor fasted," it was an altogether different matter.[34] This type of Muslim was the most effective "agent" of the West, "the open window through which the enemy climbed in,"[35] as Afghani put it. Because this type of Muslim was the product of the new education which the West introduced into Muslim society, the foreign missionary schools were denounced as the major source of intellectual and moral contamination. A distinction was made between the right kind of education and the education that led the young astray: The wrong kind was the one provided by the "foreign teachers, the Jesuits, and the Frères."[36]

Inevitably, the reformist *ulema* thus found themselves opposed not only to the reactionary traditionalists "who resisted all change," but to the young "renegades" who wanted "to westernize Islam . . . to make Muslims forget their history and abandon their heritage."[37]

Islamic reformism left a deep imprint on Arab political consciousness. Its ideology reflected pretty clearly the transitional epoch in which it flourished; it articulated the fears and hopes of a society experiencing the first pangs of change. Thanks to the reformist writers and preachers and mostly to Rida's monthly *al-Manar*, the ideology

---

[33] They were accused of wanting to lead Muslims astray: They "deceived Muslims by telling them: 'Europe discarded religion and established the secular state thus assuring progress and success. . . . Muslims will never get anywhere so long as we are under the domination of Islam.'" Shakib Arslan, *Limadha ta'akhkhar al-muslimun*, 3rd ed. (Cairo, H. 1358), p. 57.

[34] Rida, *al-Manar*, vol. IX (1906), p. 128.

[35] Rida, *Tarikh al-ustadh*, vol. I, p. 313.

[36] Rida, *al-Manar*, vol. IX (1906), p. 129.

[37] The former type is the *jamid* (ossified), the latter *jahid* (renegade). See Arslan, *Limadha ta'akhkhar al-muslimun*, p. 77.

of reformism reached wide circles throughout the Muslim world and kept alive the original impulse of Afghani and 'Abdu.

But the age of Islamic reformism was also "an age of small deeds and great compromises."[38] The compromises were made in the face of ineluctable necessity imposed by the overwhelming impact of the West. Reformism's failures were probably partly due to its inability to translate ideology into a political movement. Afghani had this in mind when, shortly before his death, he told Mughrabi that the one thing that Islamic reform lacked was an organized religious movement. Thus lacking the means that only power could bestow, the reformists were never able directly to determine the course of political events. It is against this background that the fate of the Islamic reformist movement of the Muslim Brotherhood (which emerged after World War I) may be understood. Yet despite the Brotherhood's phenomenal growth and vast mass appeal it came too late to reverse the course of history. Perhaps the main historical role of Islamic reformism was to usher in the secular epoch which it opposed but could not successfully arrest.

[38] Compare the same period in Russia, James H. Billington, *The Icon and the Axe* (New York, 1966), pp. 439ff.

Chapter IV. The Structure of Christian Intellectualism

Social Background and Psychological Orientation

The term Christian is used here in a broad sense to signify social and psychological traits rather than religious affiliation. Only in specific instances does the term refer to the religious point of view.

Christian intellectualism as a mental outlook was the product of a social and psychological process peculiar to the experience of certain Christian social strata in Syria (including Lebanon and Palestine). It was in large part the result of the transformation of Christian education in the nineteenth century and of economic and social change which the Christians pioneered. As such it received its most distinctive expression by those most affected by this change in society, i.e., the "Christian intellectuals."[1]

For the Christian Arab the Awakening was the prelude to alienation. Christian self-identity had two fundamental parts, both negative: identity in terms of religious faith (Christianity), in contradistinction to Islam; and identity in terms of sectarian affiliation, in contradistinction to other sects (e.g., Maronite and Greek Orthodox). Syria to the Christian Arab was "home" in a different sense from what it was to his fellow Muslim. Emigration presented itself as a natural outlet: life was made meaningful not within the ancestral home, but outside

---

[1] These may be divided into three main groups. The first consists of the early literati, whose principal preoccupation was linguistic and literary. Its representative and most important figures include Ahmad Faris al-Shidyaq (1804–87), Adib Ishaq, Nasif al-Yaziji (1800–1871), Ibrahim al-Yaziji (1847–1906), Qistaki al-Humsi (1858–1941), and Francis Marrash (1836–73). The second consists of those interested not only in literature and language but also in history, education, and modern knowledge. The most representative include Butrus al-Bustani (1819–93), Jurji Zaydan (1861–1914), Salim al-Bustani (1848–84), Anastathius Marie al-Karmili (1866–1947), Louis Cheikho (1859–1927), and 'Issa Iskander al-Ma'luf (1869–1956). The third group is composed of those who were concerned mostly with science, philosophy, and social and political problems. Its most important figures include Ya'qub Sarruf (1852–1927), Shibli al-Shumayyil (1860–1916), Farah Antun (1871–1922), Sulayman al-Bustani (1856–1925), Amin al-Rihani (1876–1940), Niqula Haddad (1870–1954), and Salama Musa (1887–1958).

of it. For the awakened Christian, uprootedness was a natural condition of life.[2]

The determining factor of the Christian Awakening was education. Christians were the first recipients of modern education. The missionary schools, established by the French, British, Americans, and Russians, opened their doors primarily to the Christian communities of Syria. The indigenous sectarian schools continued the old tradition of religious instruction, but they also gradually introduced western-style education. Though both sectarian and missionary schools were religiously oriented and strove to inculcate a religious (denominational) spirit into their curriculum, their system of instruction was generally rational in character, which provided the grounds for a new type of awareness. To a certain extent it encouraged independent judgment: By introducing the preliminary elements of scientific thinking, it inescapably created conditions which would loosen the hold of the traditional religious mode of thought.

The enlightenment (al-nahda) was the main rationalizing force within Christian intellectualism. It led to the social and psychological tensions that accompanied the emergence of the first modern intellectuals of Arab society. The formation of this new mentality, which began in the Christian communities of Syria, was attended by the classical opposition between the older and younger generations:[3] It is important to note that the experience of drifting away from tradi-

[2] This was expressed by one of the uprooted Christian Arabs as follows: Christians had "no attachment to the soil of Syria, no idea that Syria was the natural home of the Syrians. Rather it seemed that the best thing people who had been so unfortunate as to be born in Syria could do was to leave it as soon as they could, and adopt some other country. Many Syrians adopted spiritually some European nationality or other while they were still in Syria. Now thousands of Syrians were adopting a foreign soil as their home." Edward Atiyah, *An Arab Tells His Story* (London, 1946), p. 27.

[3] The following ancedote is illustrative of the Christian experience of the gap between the generations. It is told by Ya'qub Sarruf, one of the two editors of the scientific monthly *al-Muqtataf*. He had just returned from school to spend his vacation in his village in the Lebanese mountains, and friends of the family had come to greet him. "I informed [them] that the earth revolved around its axis. My father glared at me, but I paid no attention. He bit his lip in rage, but I wouldn't be silenced. My audience was listening to my disquisition, and everybody was laughing. (It did not occur to me that they were laughing at me.) My father could restrain himself no longer, he got up in the middle of the room and announced that what I was saying was not true, that my books were not true, that my teachers were in error. He presented as proof the fact that our door which opened out to the north had always opened out to the north and always will, that the sun which set behind the mountain of Mi'ad in the West had always set out in the West and will continue to do so. He told me to shut up. And for the time being I shut up." Text in 'Abboud, *Ruwwad,* p. 200.

tional ways was at first an exclusively Christian experience; only later did it occur within Arab Islam.

The new educated class of Christian Arabs was endowed with three types of learning which gave Christian intellectualism its distinctive character: thorough training in Arabic literature, mastery of a European language, and familiarity with modern scientific knowledge.

All the sectarian schools put great stress on the teaching of Arabic literature and grammar. Indeed, the Christian clergy had a long tradition of Arabic learning which went back to the seventeenth and eighteenth centuries. (It must be remembered that since the middle ages Arabic had been the ritual language of most of the eastern Christian churches.) The sectarian schools were strongly influenced by this tradition, and it gave their pattern of education a distinctly Arab character. Revival of Arabic classical literature was in large part a product of this cultural momentum.

Under the influence of a rational system of instruction, the teaching of Arabic in Christian schools received a systematic character. The classical language was now used for communicating the new knowledge, and thus had to be adapted to new conceptual needs. It was gradually transformed from an inert and ceremonial language into an effective vehicle of intellectual communication. In Syria, it was the Christian intellectual stratum that first came into possession of this modernized Arabic and utilized it in their writing.

Christian and foreign-run schools put equal stress on European languages, especially French and English. This equipped the educated Christians with another intellectual tool which their Muslim compatriots did not acquire until later. Knowledge of European languages profoundly influenced the orientation of the educated Christians, and it opened up new horizons for them by putting them in direct contact with European literature and learning. In this respect, the Christian awakening, unlike the Muslim, was the product of direct intellectual contact with Europe. From an objective point of view, the Christian intellectuals found themselves performing a special role in society; they became the go-between on the intellectual and economic, as well as the political, levels, which strongly influenced both their social position and their attitude.

Perhaps more important than language training was the mental outlook to which the new education gave rise. Inevitably new ideas introduced new frames of reference. In the English-speaking schools, such as the Syrian Protestant College, there was a strong trend toward a specifically scientific outlook. The humanistic and literary type of orientation was the dominant trend in the French-speaking schools—

the Jesuit College in Beirut and most of the other sectarian schools in Lebanon. The two approaches to learning, the humanistic and the scientific, were not in opposition to each other. On the contrary, despite differences in emphasis, both the Latin and the Anglo-Saxon types of education inculcated a new critical spirit which began to govern intellectual investigation, whether humanistic or scientific. Indeed, for the Christian students, the categories of the scientific approach together with the concepts of the literary approach formed a unified outlook. The "Jesuit" and the "Anglo-Saxon" mentalities were united by a common western denominator.

Christian Secular Orientation

The mental outlook characteristic of Christian intellectualism developed along lines running counter to the dogmatic premises of both Christian and Muslim traditionalism. For the educated Christian engaged in literary or economic activity the world had been "disenchanted," freed from the values and concepts which had frozen it for immemorial generations. The methodology of the classroom together with the pragmatic experience of the market place produced an attitude that no longer put much store by values and concepts based on absolute, a priori presuppositions. And if in practical life specific conditions determined particular needs, in the moral sphere the "good" was determined by particular situations. Hence "good and bad are never absolute, but relative values determined by the conditions of time and place."[4]

Christian intellectuals always eschewed direct confrontation and went out of their way to evade religious controversy. But in an unconscious, indeliberate fashion they found themselves assuming positions that were opposed to those of Islamic reformism. Christian intellectualism, starting from secular assumptions and proceeding according to secular criteria, could not steer completely clear of issues that were fundamental to reformism. Thus the Darwinist Shibli Shumayyil (d. 1916) could state that separation of church and state was essential to any kind of social progress and that it was required by social science.[5] The historian Zaydan (d. 1914) could argue that the Arabs' fitness to partake of modern civilization derived neither from their religion nor from the achievements of Islamic civilization but from qualities inherent in them as human beings.[6]

[4] Shibli al-Shumayyil, *Majmu'a* [Anthology] (Cairo, 1909–10?), vol. II, p. 85.

[5] *Ibid.*, pp. 296–97.

[6] Jurji Zaydan, *Rihla ila uruba sanat 1912* [A Trip to Europe in 1912] (Cairo, 1923), pp. 122–23.

In the Christian perspective Europe appeared in a totally different light: It was not, as for the Muslim reformists, a threat to ward off, but a model to copy. The Christian writers who now came into their own were more concerned with analyzing the ailments of society and describing its needs than with formulating defensive arguments against Europe.[7] Thus, inescapably, the ideological constructions of Islamic reformism could not have much meaningful social content for the Christian westernizing intellectual.

The Christian intellectuals upheld values and objectives presupposing a different ideological base from that of Islamic reformists. It insisted on "science" and on "modern civilization"; it sought, without directly aiming to, to break down the mental barriers that protected the traditionalist and religious reformist position. In this, one can perhaps detect an unconscious will seeking not so much the "truth" as the political transmutation of the Christian Arab situation in Muslim society. Christian intellectuals, by upholding reason and the scientific approach, were indirectly attacking the sources from which social and political authority derived its legitimacy. And, on the level of social theory, by advocating the supremacy of popular will, they struck at the very foundations of the established political order.

The rational and nonreligious frame of reference set up by the Christian intellectuals projected their refusal to accept the prevailing valuational claims and represented a rebellion against the established culture and social order. This was embodied in the central drive of Christian writers to secularize social existence by secularizing thought. Again, they instinctively knew that, without secularizing the view of history and the foundations on which society and the state were built, it would be impossible to solve the problem of Christian estrangement in Arab society. Christian intellectualism may thus be viewed as an effort to rehabilitate the Christian Arab in his Muslim environment.

But the educated Christians did not have open to them the same avenues of action as were open to Muslims. It must be remembered that Christian intellectuals generally had no fixed political loyalties; and having no vested interests in the status quo they were always ready to take up the pen in defense of any position with which they empathized or from which they derived benefit. Not surprisingly,

[7] Instead of stressing the Muslim or Arab contributions to Europe, the Christian intellectuals emphasized the more practical issues at hand. These words by Salim al-Bustani (d. 1884) typify the Christian attitude: "Instead of constantly bragging about ourselves and our great past, let us try to find out something about our condition." "Man nahnu?" [Who are We?], *Majali al-ghurar li kuttab al-qarn al-tasi' 'ashar* [An Anthology of Nineteenth Century Writers], ed. Yusuf Sufayr (Beirut, 1906), p. 100.

therefore, there was not any one political attitude with which the Christian intellectuals as a group could be identified.

Probably the most common Christian tendency was to withdraw from political commitment of any kind. This was especially true of those who lived in the Ottoman Empire—particularly during the period of Hamidian rule (1876–1908), when all intellectual energies had perforce to be channeled into literary and educational activities. Thus the influential Butrus al-Bustani (d. 1883), his son Salim, and their associates in Beirut devoted themselves to teaching, publishing a newspaper, and putting out an encyclopedia. Others concentrated on composing poetry and compiling dictionaries.

Engagement in politics, though rare, was the second alternative and was undertaken by some of the Christians. The activities of Ahmad Faris al-Shidyaq (d. 1887) and Sulayman al-Bustani (d. 1925), two of the most prominent Christian intellectuals of the late Ottoman epoch, represent two different types of political engagement. Shidyaq, after a long and checkered career in Europe and North Africa, settled in Constantinople in 1861 and published a newspaper (*al-Jawa'ib*), in which for over twenty years he fully supported the principles and policies of Ottomanism. Bustani, who translated the *Iliad* into Arabic, was a bitter enemy of Hamidian rule; he gave his backing to the Young Turk regime which overthrew Abdul Hamid in 1908. In 1914, a few months before the outbreak of the war, he was appointed to a cabinet post, the highest office ever to be occupied by a Christian of his generation. A third type of political involvement that was quite common in the pre-World War I years was that experienced by Khalil Ghanim (d. 1903), a Maronite member of the Ottoman Parliament, which was abolished by Abdul Hamid in 1876. Ghanim took refuge in France and produced vigorous anti-Ottoman propaganda. He was an active member of the Young Turk movement during the period when opposition to Ottoman rule had begun to spread among Arab Muslims. The idea of nationalism had already begun to make its appearance in the Arab provinces of the Ottoman Empire and many educated Christians found it possible to identify with Arabism, to which they sought to give a secular, nonreligious orientation.

For those Christians who emigrated to Egypt a wider range of political participation was possible. Under British rule the Lebanese and Syrian Christian writers and journalists enjoyed broad freedom of expression on all the social and political subjects prohibited in the Ottoman Empire. They generally favored British rule, a fact which placed them in a bad position with the Egyptian nationalists. They also tended to be anti-Ottoman, while nationalists in Egypt viewed the

Ottoman Empire as an ally. Though most of them did not participate actively in political life, they exercised considerable political influence through the periodical press, which to a large extent they controlled.

Christian Intellectualism and the West

The evolution of the myth of the West in Christian intellectualism paralleled that of true Islam in Islamic reformism. For the Christian intellectual Europe and its civilization represented the same kind of ideal as the Golden Age did for the Islamic reformists. This parallelism should not be stretched too far, however. The Christian intellectuals did not derive a principle of reform based on westernization. In the strict sense of the word, an explicit westernizing ideology did not emerge from the Christian modernist outlook as did a reformist ideology from Islamic reformism.

Though the Christian intellectuals did not feel driven to justify westernization, they nevertheless felt compelled to give an account of why the West was to be emulated. They singled out certain virtues Europeans possessed as a result of European "progress" and "civilization."[8] Some did acknowledge the West's cultural indebtedness to the Arabs, but the stress was always on the secular aspects.[9]

The fact that western culture was a Christian culture could not be overlooked. This constituted a problem for which there was no easy solution. It brought Christian intellectuals into natural harmony with European ways and values, while it constituted a barrier for the Muslims. The emphasis on the secular aspect of western culture was not sufficient to dispel the underlying antagonism between Islam and the West. True, Christian writers always stressed the fact that they regarded themselves as Arabs (and "easterners") first, but this did not overcome the problem of religious affiliation. This inherent bond

---

[8] These virtues were very clear. "Let every Easterner admit that Westerners enjoy many virtues which he may copy with profit, such as straightforwardness, trustworthiness, truthfulness, perseverence in work, promptness, good companionship, cleanliness . . ." al-Hilal, vol. III (1895), p. 699. Zaydan distinguished the good qualities from the bad ones. "The good qualities which may be emulated are: knowing one's duty, keeping appointments and being on time, cultivation of public morals through sound education, the education and social cultivation of women, advancement of education and the enhancement of literary production, work and perseverence. As to what should be evaded in European culture: too much freedom . . . in particular sexual freedom, freedom of the working classes, everything that violates the sense of Eastern modesty, lukewarmness toward religion and open atheism which lead to ruin . . ." Rihla, p. 47.

[9] Shidyaq maintained that "anyone who has known Europe also knows that there is really no difference between us and Europeans; neither in the power of reason, nor in the power of understanding, nor in the power of intelligence . . . nor in any other natural attribute." al-Jawa'ib (May 12, 1868).

with the Christian nations of Europe expressed itself in many ways, most decisively in the political sphere. Did not Christians always look to Europe for protection? When the chips were down, did not the European powers always come to the rescue of the eastern Christians —for example, in Lebanon in 1860?

Christian intellectualism, to free itself from this relationship, had to stress the secular view of man and society, to make clear the distinction between the religious and the secular. Many Christian intellectuals went out of their way to align themselves against the threat of European imperialism; many ardently upheld the principle of Arab nationalism. Even though, from the Christian intellectual's point of view, Europe may have been regarded as a threat in terms of power, it was still considered primarily as the home of civilization in terms of thought. In Muslim eyes Europe appeared as a political and military threat; in the Christian view it emerged as the bearer of the true intellectual tradition.

The Problem of Borrowing

It was impossible for the Christian Arab not to wish for a way to westernize society. Theoretically there could be no limit to what the Arabs might borrow from the West. To the Christians, the Islamic reformists' limitations on borrowing could not be valid. Nevertheless, Christian intellectuals had to be especially aware of these limitations and reservations, and they always tried to see the West with Muslim eyes in order to determine these limits. These conditions determined the scope of the Christian intellectual contribution.

In dealing with the problem of what to borrow from the West, Christian intellectualism singled out three elements: scientific knowledge, industry, and constitutional government. The Christian writers argued that without science the possession of any kind of power was impossible. The West owed its material superiority above all to science. Moreover, in order to become part of the modern world it was essential to acquire the scientific secrets of the West. Here, the Christian intellectuals did not go beyond advocating the practical need for scientific knowledge. Science as a prerequisite for a radical mental transformation was hardly discussed, but new scientific theories and discoveries inspired considerable interest. The few writers who tried to deal with the philosophical implications of the scientific outlook kept their distance from the central religious issues and dealt with generalities expressed in broad terms.[10]

[10] See p. 63.

Modern industry was viewed by the Christian westernizing intellectuals as a necessary condition not only for economic growth but for reform in all spheres. Industrialization was the hallmark of modern civilization. Christian intellectualism tried to allay the fears expressed by the Islamic reformists, who, though outwardly enthusiastic about radical economic change, harbored great misgivings about the social and political implications. The Christian intellectuals had little objection to Europeans investing in Arab lands; they welcomed European capital and modern techniques, believing their effects to be beneficial both economically and socially. The Islamic reformists, on the other hand, were reluctant to accept this view, though they did not directly oppose it. They felt that by encouraging European investment they were opening the way for European interference in their internal affairs and for unpredictable social innovation. While Christian intellectualism favored modern industry for its socially transforming effects, Islamic reformism admitted its economic necessity but opposed it for fear of its social and political consequences.

Christian writers were practically unanimous in advocating the introduction of representative government. In this perhaps more than in any other realm the need for borrowing was put in unqualified terms. Contributing to the open and full espousal of western political reforms was the knowledge of the Islamic reformist's verbal support for democratic government. Thus, whether anglophiles or admirers of the French tradition, the Christian westernizers declared themselves fully in favor of a political system based on democracy and constitutional government.

In their liberal outlook, the Christian intellectuals reflected not only a Christian propensity but also the concrete interests of their social group. This position expressed the sentiments and interests of the emerging Christian bourgeoisie in Egypt and Syria. Thus, the Christian intellectuals, like the liberal European intelligentsia of the nineteenth century, posited laissez-faire economics and parliamentarianism as fundamental principles of progress. Though the Arab Christians did not directly criticize Islam's identification of the secular and religious realms, they did so implicitly. They thus indirectly questioned the viability of the caliphal form of government in the modern world.[11]

---

[11] Republicanism was not openly advocated until toward the end of the nineteenth century. One of the important open calls for the republican form of government was made by Jubra'il al-Dallal (d. 1892) in an article entitled "Republican Rule: When?" Partial text in Kayyali, al-Adab, p. 62.

The Problem of Reform

In its theoretical formulations Christian intellectualism appeared committed to the principle of borrowing, but when it came to the problem of implementation, of translating ideas into concrete acts, it took a rather diffident attitude. The Christian bourgeois intellectuals were committed to ideas more than they were to a specific social program. With few exceptions—largely in education and the periodical press, where they played active roles—the Christian intellectuals were all theoreticians. Those Christians who were engaged in direct political action were either officials for the established authority (e.g., Sulayman Bustani) or followers in Muslim-led movements.[12] In either case they were always in subordinate positions.

Moreover, the idea of reform as understood by the Christian writers was in many respects radically different from that elaborated by the reformist *ulemas*. Essentially, the Christian concept referred to something concrete. Reform in the literal sense of the word (i.e., *islah:* correction, repair) signified both moral and material change. The Christian intellectuals generally showed great mistrust of extravagant plans for reform, and, like the conservative European middle class, they tended to scorn utopianism.

Christian intellectualism was generally in favor of gradualism as a method of change: Matters should take their course, and viable change should come only slowly.[13] Whenever confronted by political realities, Christian intellectualism abstained from supporting any kind of radicalism.[14] The attitude of most Christian intellectuals toward social and political reform remained essentially nonviolent.

Another aspect of the Christian view of reform lay in its critical rationalism. It attacked blind attachment to established custom as essentially regressive. It contrasted the "movement of thought in the West" with "intellectual immobility" in Arab society.[15] This attitude provided the grounds for a critical approach having some of the

[12] For examples of this type of participation, see chap. VII.

[13] This position, reminiscent of that taken by 'Abdu for different reasons, was clearly outlined by Jurji Zaydan in 1908: "We should be wise to concentrate our efforts on educating the nation and training it to accomplish its tasks and leave it for our children and grandchildren to decide what goals they wish to set up for themselves. If they wanted independence then they should achieve it themselves; or if they wanted a constitutional government they should also establish it themselves." *Mukhtarat,* vol. III, p. 5.

[14] For important exceptions, see pp. 84–86.

[15] For example, Adib Ishaq said: "Vision has become so blinded by the delusion of perfection of traditional beliefs . . . that the movement of thought in the West has become totally obscured from it. Westerners move forward and we remain standing where we are." Text in *Majali,* ed. Sufayr, p. 168.

elements of systematic analysis. But Christian intellectualism failed to elaborate this position and its rational implications in specific terms. Such elaboration would have entailed headlong collision with the Islamic reformist trend. Indeed such collision would have been inevitable given the Christians' position that secularization of outlook (or an absolutist frame of reference) was the precondition for the adoption of a rational and coherent system of thought and evaluation. This is why Christian intellectualism had frequently to conceal its position behind broad generalizations.

The Idea of History

The idea of history in reformist ideology was a shallow notion which served to organize its views of reality around the dominant myth of Islam's Golden Age. Christian intellectualism, on the other hand, was "critical" rather than "mythical" (to use Cassirer's terminology) in its view of history. From the Christian point of view, the historical constructions of Islamic reformism were not only objectively untenable, but, what is more important, religiously exclusive.

Islamic reformism's vision of history provided the scheme for defining its system of values. For Christian intellectualism, consciousness of history signified a deliberate, conscious act, an advance into a precise dimension of time. Christian Arabs could claim two traditions: (1) the (local) sectarian tradition and (2) the Christian tradition as a whole (including western and eastern orthodox Christianity). Thus in terms of Islamic tradition, the Christian was an "outsider" in the same sense that he was an outsider socially in Muslim society. For the Christian intellectual, the central problem was to find a position in history outside the religious realm. Christian intellectualism established a secular position from which it sought to reconcile the opposition between the strictly Christian and the strictly Islamic views. The reconciliation it suggested based itself on substituting for the idea of the Golden Age the idea of civilization. From here it was only one more step to view Islamic civilization from a secular, Arab stance.

The Christian view of history never explicitly advanced a critique of the religious approach to history. It nevertheless underscored the values and concepts with which such a critique could be undertaken. In this respect, Christian intellectualism struck the first blow in demythologizing the historical conception set forth by Islamic reformism.

It was only natural that the Christian Arab intellectual would emphasize the distinction between Arab and Muslim. Elements that in reformist thought were considered religious constituted for the Christian the essence of what should be viewed as secular. Those elements contributed most to the estrangement of the Christian Arab in Muslim society. The Christian intellectuals had to establish a de facto distinction between the religious and secular realms if only to establish a common ground where Christian and Muslim could meet. This trend is seen most clearly in the literary and humanistic character of Christian thought during this period.

It is probably correct to state that Arab national self-consciousness owes its inception to the effort of secularizing Arab history by the Christian intellectuals. Indeed, one should remember that Arabism has its roots not in the theory of Islamic revivalism elaborated by Islamic reformism, but rather in the Christian suprareligious definition of Arab society and cultural traditions. Islam itself was considered as a factor of the cultural evolution and evaluated as an Arab cultural contribution. Implicitly, Islam did not comprise the totality of Arab cultural achievement. In these terms the distinction between Arab and Muslim received its first concrete determination.

The Idea of Nationalism

The secular conception of nationalism was in large part an outcome of Christian intellectualism's striving to rationalize Islamic history and to define the Christian Arab's relation to it. Christian political thought, faithful to the secular impulses which animated it, postulated the idea of social unity rather than that of (religious) community as the basis of the idea of *watan* (fatherland). "Love of fatherland is part of faith," declared Butrus al-Bustani;[16] and Adib Ishaq added: "Devotion to the fatherland makes us all brothers"[17] (i.e., not just Muslims and Christians). Ishaq was probably the first Christian intellectual to resurrect Ibn Khaldun's concept of *'asabiyyah* (devotion, esprit de corps) and to define it in terms of "patriotism and nationalism."[18] He was probably also the first to use the nationalist slogan, "Long live the nation, long live the fatherland," which he derived from the French revolutionary tradition.[19]

[16] He used this as the emblem of his short-lived paper *Nafir Suriyya* (1860–61). The term "fatherland" was used by both Tahtawi and Khayr al-Din Pasha, but did not carry quite the same meaning. Loyalty to the fatherland to Tahtawi was understood in religious terms, to the latter it lacked definite territorial designation.

[17] Ishaq was among the first writers to stress the element of language as a basis of Arab brotherhood. See 'Abboud, *Ruwwad,* p. 188.

[18] *Ibid.*

[19] He first used it in 1887 in an article published in his newspaper, *Misr.* Text 'Abboud, *Ruwwad,* pp. 97–98.

Of what nation, of what fatherland did the Christian intellectuals speak? On this there was a good deal of disagreement. Shidyaq, for example, came close to forming an idea of Ottoman nationalism based on administrative reform and on the brotherhood of all subjects within the Ottoman Empire regardless of religion or ethnic origin. (This concept was revived in slightly different fashion after 1908 and took the form of a political movement calling for political equality in a decentralized Ottoman Empire.)[20] Butrus Bustani, on the other hand, thought in terms of the Syrian nation and applied the idea of nationalism to the Syrian fatherland (geographic Syria), thus coming close to forming an idea of Syrian nationalism. Ishaq went further by referring to a broader concept of nation, of an Arab nation, or at least of an Arabic-speaking group of nations: "We are joined to one another by the bond of language."[21] In his writings we encounter the first clear expression of the idea of Arab nationhood.

There also developed among some Christian intellectuals, particularly in Lebanon, a current of thought which more and more came to regard Lebanon as a separate entity. However, the notion of a Lebanese "nationalism" did not develop until after World War I, with the establishment under the French mandate of an "independent" Greater Lebanon.

Even though the Christian writers may not have provided final solutions, their grappling with these problems supplied the concepts, vocabulary, and general framework that paved the way for the rising educated generation to move away from the ideas of Islam and pan-Islamism and toward a more secular view of society.

[20] See chap. VII.
[21] 'Abboud, Ruwwad, p. 188.

Chapter V. The Social Ideology of Christian Intellectualism

The Westernization of Ideas

Given its starting points, Christian intellectualism was bound to follow a course of increasing rationalization. This can be seen in (1) the tendency to move away from purely literary and linguistic preoccupations, which characterized the first stage of the Arab Awakening; and (2) the tendency to become more concerned with social and political issues. There is no doubt that the progressive rationalization of Christian thought was in large part due to its increasing westernization, which involved western ideas and habits of thought and their application to the social existential situation. Preoccupation with social and political problems gave rise to social and political orientations which allow us to speak of a distinctively Christian "social ideology." Before analyzing the substantive content of this ideology —which has greatly influenced twentieth-century Arab thought— we must first define more clearly the process of intellectual westernization.

Two currents of European thought had perhaps the greatest formative impact on Christian intellectualism in terms of basic method: (1) the rational and liberal tradition of the Enlightenment (and to a lesser extent revolutionary and postrevolutionary France); and (2) the nineteenth-century tradition of positivism and liberalism (and social Darwinism). Not until the end of the nineteenth century did any other major current of European thought make itself as strongly felt.

The Enlightenment had a tremendous impact on the educated Christians of this generation.[1] The greatest influence was probably exerted by Montesquieu, Rousseau, and Voltaire. Montesquieu offered insights into social reality that were really revolutionary. And his relativistic approach hit a responsive chord in a stratum driven by

[1] This section is based on an analysis of major articles published in Bustani's encyclopedia, *Da'irat al-ma'arif*, and in three leading journals: *al-Muqtataf*, founded by Ya'qub Sarruf and Faris Nimr in Beirut in 1876, moved to Cairo in 1884; Zaydan's *al-Hilal*, founded in Cairo in 1892; and Antun's *al-Jami'a*, published in Cairo from 1899 to 1905 and in New York between 1906 and 1908.

the impulse to free itself from restrictive, oppressive absolutes. The idea that "particular needs and specific circumstances," "time and space," were basic determining factors of laws and constitutions provided a wholly fresh vantage point from which to understand history and society.[2] Montesquieu's elaboration of the separation of powers contributed another revealing idea with revolutionary implications not only for the existing political system but also for the theoretical foundations of the traditional Islamic view of society and the state. The Christian intellectuals were influenced by Montesquieu in still another way. The spirit of toleration that permeated his writings, especially *Les Lettres Persanes,* pointed to a radically new way of looking at things. It showed how great were the benefits to be gained from the mutual toleration of differences.

The impact of Rousseau's ideas is more difficult to assess. Certainly the concepts of "popular sovereignty" and "general will" made their mark; these ideas appear again and again in the early articles and discussions of *al-Muqtataf* and *al-Hilal.* They are later used in combination with other ideas such as "natural right" and the "rights of man" as slogans favoring constitutional and representative government. Rousseau, however, seems to have been difficult to assimilate systematically. His influence remained uneven: the impact of *Contrat Social,* which was enthusiastically read in French as well as in Arabic, was probably owing more to its tone rather than to its content. This work had a strong emotional appeal, and it generated much enthusiasm for Rousseau's more romantic aspects.

Voltaire was perhaps the most influential of the three. His critical spirit and his philosophical and religious toleration held special appeal to the young educated Christian Arabs. Perhaps his strongest influence derived from his anticlericalism. The anticlerical tendency to be found in most Christian intellectuals was surprisingly strong. It manifested itself in different forms, but mainly in criticism of religious bigotry and intolerance. The best attacks against the backwardness and corruption of institutional religion (from Shidyaq to Gibran[3]) were expressed in typically Voltairian vocabulary. The Christian intellectuals were much impressed by Voltaire's skeptical spirit, but failed to draw final conclusions that could be articulated in a coherently skeptical position. There remained a residual conformist strain in the attitude of Christian intellectuals which inhibited radical doubt.

Nineteenth-century middle class liberalism held profound attraction for the rising educated class in Egypt and the Fertile Crescent,

[2] See Bustani, Introduction to *Da'irat al-ma'arif,* vol. I (1876), p. 2.
[3] Kahlil Gibran (d. 1932), author of *The Prophet.*

particularly for the educated Christians. The ideas of political liberty, property, free enterprise, and limited government, which characterized liberal thought in England (Bentham and Mill) and postrevolutionary France (Royer-Collar and Benjamin Constant), were reflected in the political writings of the Christian intellectuals. It is revealing that the ideas of conservative thought (de Maistre, de Bonald, and Lamennais) and of radical thought (St. Simon, Fourier, Blanc, and Proudhon) had little impact.[4] And it is interesting to note that while the great revolution of 1789 figured largely in Christian political writing, the revolutions of 1830 and 1848—and their social and political implications—are rarely mentioned.

Among French writers of the nineteenth century who aroused special interest were August Comte, Ernest Renan, and Gustave Le Bon. It is doubtful that the first two were read to any large extent. The main ideas of Comte's positive philosophy and Renan's philosophical and historical works were obtained mostly from secondhand sources, such as the leading periodical, *Revue des Deux Mondes.* Comte's special appeal was his "scientific" view of society and the comprehensive solutions he suggested for the betterment of the human condition. He was also well received for the secular theology which his positivism afforded the Christian intellectuals, who, like all rebels against tradition, longed for new grounds of certitude. Renan engendered special interest because of his dominant position in French thought and because of his theories concerning Islam and Christianity, which many Christian intellectuals found highly plausible.[5] Farah Antun (d. 1922), from the intellectual point of view probably the most westernized of the Christian intellectuals, gave the most systematic presentation of Renan's ideas. Le Bon caught the attention of the educated elite toward the end of the century partly because of his interest in Islam and partly because of his social psychological theories, particularly his *Psychologie des Foules* (Paris, 1895), which was one of his first works to be translated into Arabic and to become popular.

Among the English writers of the nineteenth century, Mill, Darwin, Spencer, and Huxley exerted the greatest influence, particularly on the Christians trained in British or American schools. They welcomed the idea of individual liberty found in J. S. Mill's works. His doctrine

[4] Reference was often made to Littré and Berthelot; Guizot also seems to have been known to most Christian intellectuals. General reference to the early socialists was made by Jurji Zaydan. See Zaydan, *Mukhtarat,* vol. II, pp. 88–91.

[5] Particularly those set forth in *L'Islamisme et la science* (Paris, 1883); and *Histoire des origines du Christianisme* (Paris, 1863–83).

of political liberty served to confirm and to strengthen their belief in the principle of social and religious toleration. Mill's political ideas gained great vogue among the readers and contributors of the Christian periodicals, and his liberalism became a dominant current in Christian political thought.

Darwinism was introduced into Arabic by Shibli Shumayyil, who adopted the Darwinist creed while still a medical student at the Syrian Protestant College in Beirut (he graduated in 1871).[6] He derived his social Darwinist theories from Ludwig Büchner (d. 1899), the German materialist philosopher who was presented to Arab readers by Shumayyil as "the foremost exponent of Darwinian philosophy."[7] Owing to his scientific training, Shumayyil's analysis of Darwin's ideas was among the most precise and comprehensive interpretations of European writers ever made by Christian intellectualism. In 1910 he published a book on Darwin's theory of evolution which he entitled *The Philosophy of Evolution and Progress,* and he wrote numerous articles which appeared in *al-Muqtataf* and *al-Hilal* over a period of three decades. He influenced other writers who also contributed articles on the social and philosophical meaning of Darwin's scientific discoveries. It is interesting to note that the controversy which raged between the Darwinists and the anti-Darwinists during the last decade of the nineteenth century and the early part of the twentieth raised practically all the major problems that were raised a generation earlier by English Victorian intellectuals.[8]

Herbert Spencer was accorded special honors by the Christian intellectuals as *the* philosopher of modern science. He represented a "synthesis of the thought of Comte and the thought of Darwin," which enabled Christian writers to examine more closely the relevance of science and scientific theories to society and social problems. Spencer, moreover, gave clarity and focus to Comte's positivism and rendered Darwinism more meaningful by translating the theories of both writers into a concrete social system bridging the gap between natural science and the science of society. As a result of Spencer's writings, the ideas of evolution, social progress, struggle for survival, and survival of the fittest became the slogans of the new scientific ideology of the enlightened "modernists." Thanks to Spencer, Darwinism became a philosophic doctrine "beyond dispute," and Spencer

[6] In 1882 an instructor at this college was forced to resign because of his Darwinist views; see Hourani, *Arabic Thought,* pp. 249–50.

[7] Shumayyil read a French translation of Büchner's major work, *Darwinismus und Socialismus* (1894).

[8] See "Charles Darwin," *al-Muqtataf,* vol. VII (1882), pp. 2–6; and "al-Madhhab al-darwini" [Darwinist Doctrine], *ibid.,* pp. 65–72; 121–27.

himself was declared "one of the greatest European philosophers, if not the greatest philosopher of all ages."[9]

With new translations other intellectual influences made themselves felt. In *al-Hilal, al-Muqtataf,* and other periodicals we find increasing references to works ranging from Plato to Nietzsche. For example, Zaydan, writing in 1908, makes reference in one page to Plato's *Republic,* More's *Utopia* (1518), Campanella's *Civitas Solis* (1623), Bacon's *New Atlantis* (1627), and Fenelon's *Les Aventures de Télémaque* (1694).[10] In *al-Muqtataf,* with its concentration on science, the most recent scientific theories and discoveries were carefully presented and analyzed. In *al-Jami'a* Antun was the first to introduce previously unknown European writers,[11] such as Marx and Tolstoy; and he was the first to translate Nietzsche.[12] His impact on the emerging youth may be assessed from the following remark by Salamah Musa, who himself later became a leading Christian intellectual in Egypt.

> In 1905 . . . literature consisted for us of dead grammar, of the rules of rhetoric and style, which we had to learn by heart. . . . It was therefore a revelation to discover Farah Antun's *al-Jami'a.* . . . I bought all the works of this great writer and through him discovered the world of European literature which we didn't know existed.[13]

The Grounds of Certainty

A central concern of Christian thought was to form a "scientific" view of reality. The Christian generation which came to maturity between the publication of the first volume of Butrus Bustani's *Encyclopedia* (1875) and the appearance of the last number of Antun's *al-Jami'a* (1908) saw not only the break away from traditionalism and its narrow outlook but also the breakthrough into a new way of thinking and valuation. For this generation the dominant concern was to elucidate the bases of the new way of thinking and seeing.

[9] See Salamah Musa, "Nietzsche wal-masih" [Nietzsche and Christ] *al-Muqtataf,* vol. XXXIV (1909), p. 571; also Ya'qub Sarruf, *Fatat misr* [Egypt's Daughter], 4th ed. (Cairo, 1922), p. 47.

[10] Zaydan, *Mukhtarat,* vol. I, p. 97.

[11] For six years (1899–1905) *al-Jami'a* appeared in Cairo. In 1905 Antun emigrated to the United States, and *al-Jami'a* was published in New York from 1906 to 1908, when Antun, disillusioned, decided to return to Egypt.

[12] The first translations, which Antun made from the French, appeared in *al-Jami'a* in Cairo, "Mukhtarat min falsafat Nietzsche" [Selections from Nietzsche's Philosophy], *al-Jami'a* (1908), pp. 57–64; 81–86; 125–28. In New York Antun published a brief analysis of Nietzsche's philosophy, "al-Faylasuf Nietzsche wa falsafatuhu" [Nietzsche and His Philosophy], *ibid.,* pp. 16–17.

[13] *Tarbiyat Salamah Musa* [The Education of Salama Musa] (Cairo, 1947), pp. 112–13. In 1909 Musa introduced Schopenhauer to the Arabic reading public; for his comments on *The World as Will and Idea,* see *al-Muqtataf,* vol. XXXV (1909), pp. 989–90.

The more the Christian intellectuals became familiar with European science the more scientism dominated their mental outlook. This is one reason why Christian intellectualism developed a distinctively "scientific" idiom in Arabic.

Elaboration of clear and logical concepts came gradually. But by the turn of the century, Antun and Shumayyil had established themselves as the leading spokesmen of the new way of thought, and the groundwork of Christian intellectualism had been laid. Antun summarized the new method in Bacon's classical terms: rational proof rests on "experience, observation, and verification."[14] He was probably the first Christian writer publicly to call for a rational (i.e., scientific) interpretation of the Qur'an. He put forth this demand in the course of a controversy with 'Abdu in which he invoked the authority of Ibn Rushd (Averröes) to demonstrate the possibility of such an interpretation of Muslim dogma. "Those sections of the Qur'an," he said, "which appear to be contrary to evidence or to logical reason" should be "reinterpreted" (ta'wil),[15] pushing the theory of ijtihad to its logical limit.

Shumayyil went a step further in defining scientific validity. He developed what may be considered the most coherent materialist position in Christian Arab thought. For him it was not sufficient to base truth on purely "logical" grounds. Ultimate validity consisted in scientific (verifiable) validity. Truly valid knowledge was attainable through the method of physical science, the only kind of knowledge which can be described as scientific. He made a clear distinction between science (natural or physical science) and what he called the human sciences (al-'ulum al-bashariyya), using much the same terms as Comte's in differentiating between "physical science" and "social physics." Under Büchner's influence, Shumayyil subordinated the human sciences to the physical sciences.[16]

---

[14] See, for example, Antun's article, "Renan wa afkaruhu al-'aja'ib" [Renan and His Amazing Ideas], al-Jami'a, vol. III (1902), p. 620.

[15] Farah Antun, "Ibn Rushd wa falsaftuhu" [Ibn Rushd and His Philosophy], Muqtatafat min atharihi [Selection from His Writings] (Beirut, 1951), p. 136; also see his reply to 'Abdu, "Radd al-Jami'a 'ala radd al-imam al-jalil 'ala maqalat al-Jami'a fi Ibn Rushd" [al-Jami'a's Reply to the Imam's ['Abdu's] Comment on al-Jami'a's Article on Ibn Rushd], al-Jami'a, vol. III (1902), pp. 626–39.

[16] Thus, he wrote, natural science "is the source of all the sciences. It constitutes the grounding of the human sciences; they must precede everything else . . ." al-Muqtataf, vol. XXXIV (1909), p. 287. Shumayyil was the first to resort to psychological criteria of analysis. See his quite original study, "Abdul Hamid from the Medical Point of View: A Physiological and Psychological Study" (in ibid., pp. 565–70), where he developed the thesis that Abdul Hamid was not altogether responsible for his actions, and that many of his deeds were determined by psychological factors beyond his control.

This is not to say that the methodology elaborated by Antun and Shumayyil was adopted by all Christian intellectuals; the literary sensibility, with its humanistic and subjectivist tendencies, remained a strong current in Christian thought and continued to color much of its output. This literary, nonscientific trend affected the development of Christian thought in two ways: it inhibited the growth of truly critical analysis, and it served to perpetuate psychological dependency on "higher authority." For many Christian intellectuals "science" became precisely such "authority." Science as such was not transformed into an ingrained mental characteristic; it was not institutionalized.[17] Only recently in Arab society has scientism—the enthusiasm for science—started to mature into a theoretical and technical discipline, and it is still in its first stages.

Secularization of Thought

The scientific rationalism of Christian intellectualism—however broadly it may be defined—made possible the establishment of radical points of departure which aided the secularization of thought in the early years of the twentieth century. Its basic assumptions, even though not fully elaborated, contributed to the progressive disintegration of the foundations of traditional and, specifically, religious, convictions. It became fashionable among the educated to ridicule the backwardness and superstition of traditional arguments. A vague kind of antagonism toward everything pertaining to the older, traditional generation became current among the more outspoken intellectuals, including Muslims. Religion, in the light of the new way of looking at the world, encountered skepticism on a wide scale.

Most Christian intellectuals, far from reacting against the materialistic conception of the world presented by European positivist rationalism, accepted the unity of a physical universe governed by immanent and unchanging laws, free from supernatural control. This was precisely the trend of thought that Islamic reformism had feared and expended so much energy in combating. Afghani had defined this materialist doctrine as *al-nayshariyya* (i.e., naturalism)[18] and described it as the great heresy of the modern age.[19]

---

[17] In this respect compare the styles of 'Abdu's *Risalat al-Tawhid* (Cairo, 1897), English translation by Kenneth Cragg and Ishaq Musa'ad, *The Theology of Unity* (London, 1966), with Shumayyil's *Falsafat al-nushu' w'al-irtiqa'* [The Philosophy of Evolution and Progress] (Cairo, 1910).

[18] In his words: "*al-nayshar* [nature] is the word for nature (*tabi'a*). The doctrine of *nayshar* is derived from the doctrine of materialism [or naturalism] which made its appearance in Greece in the fourth and third centuries B.C. The purpose of this doctrine is to destroy religion and to establish communism . . ." See Mughrabi, *al-Afghani*, p. 71.

[19] He and his followers had been wholly negative in their approach to this

The avowed aim of the Christian intellectuals—those who in their articles in *al-Hilal, al-Muqtataf,* and *al-Jami'a* upheld the sovereignty of science—was to "harmonize" faith with science. Of course, from a Christian position this was quite possible, but it was not so easy for the Muslims. The ideas put forth by Christian writers after 1900, no matter how guarded and prescribed they may have been, served to pave the way for more candid expressions of naturalist and material- ist formulations.

What were some of these formulations? Ya'qub Sarruf, co-editor of *al-Muqtataf,* was one of the earliest writers to spread this scientific approach. He expressed himself in an objective and detached manner, which strengthened his influence. Under his auspices, *al-Muqtataf* maintained an exclusively scientific character: Sarruf seized every opportunity to emphasize the contrast between "scientific" truth and "metaphysical" or "imaginary" truth. He approached religion in terms of its instrumental value, not in terms of its substantive asser- tions. His view of reality was unmistakably rationalistic.[20] According to him, for example, society is governed by scientifically definable laws of "association and conflict," which are inherent in social struc- ture. Morality is a function of social control; and its motive force is religion. Since man is "more inclined to do evil than good, something is needed to incline him more toward good; this something is reli- gion."[21] Sarruf's impact was widespread because, in addition to main- taining an objective and "scientific" attitude, he refused to engage in polemics.

Shumayyil and Antun provide the best examples of the naturalist or materialist position. Shumayyil was uncompromising in his for- mulation and insisted that the scientific materialist conception was a view relating not only to a section of reality but to all reality. Materialism constituted a total world view, a systematic philosophy "founded on scientific principles with the validity of mathematics."[22] Unlike Sarruf, Shumayyil was outspoken and polemical in his ap-

---

problem. It is doubtful whether they fully grasped the scientific and philosophic principles on which the doctrine of naturalism was based and which had so much appeal for the Christian intellectuals. By the time these naturalistic theories became widespread (ca. 1900), Islamic reformism had become alien- ated from the mainstream of scientific and philosophical thought. Caught in a dead end, it had to seek refuge in the tautological formulation from which no fruitful solution could henceforth issue: "Between *true* religion and *true* science there can be no real disagreement . . ." See *al-Muqtataf,* vol. IX (1884), p. 182.

[20] E.g., see *al-Muqtataf,* vol. IX (1885), pp. 712–19.

[21] *Ibid.,* p. 718.

[22] Shibli al-Shumayyil, "Falsafat al-maddiyya wa madhhab al-nushu' " [The Philosophy of Materialism and the Theory of Evolution], *al-Muqtataf,* vol. XXXIV (1910), p. 647.

proach. With him it was as though patience were spent and truth had to be expressed.[23] Until his death in 1916 Shumayyil was one of the most controversial writers of his time.

Antun's primary aim was not only to assert the validity of the naturalist view but to justify it and make it acceptable, particularly to his Muslim contemporaries. He used Ibn Rushd to get at an adequate terminology and to establish a rationalist framework indigenous to Islamic thought. With subtlety and patience he wove argument after argument in *al-Jami'a* to show that though God was unknowable directly, contact (*ittisal*) with the divine reality was nevertheless possible. Using Ibn Rushd's terminology, he asked: "How can man reach a knowledge of God?" And his answer was: Not by "prayer and meditation [but by] continual study and research to unveil the mystery of the universe." Science is the path of knowing God; scientific truth is the ground of religious truth. Antun made a great effort to show that Ibn Rushd, "the greatest philosopher of Islam," paved the way to this knowledge and provided the means of achieving it. He sought to convince his readers that the philosophy of Ibn Rushd was essentially, like modern naturalism, "a materialist philosophy based on science."[24]

The main concern of Sarruf, Shumayyil, and Antun, as well as that of a few other Christian intellectuals who followed in their steps, was to move men's attention away from religion and metaphysics and back to the problems of the real world. They were convinced that traditionalist obscurantism and mystification must be eliminated in order to bring about intellectual enlightenment. This awareness made their assertions bolder, more explicit. Though none of them professed open atheism, they exhibited in their writings the unmistakable waning of religious belief. For these Christian intellectuals it was not quite a matter, as Nietzsche put it, of "sacrificing God to nothingness," but merely of sacrificing an untenable old truth for a valid new one. Unconsciously they were advocating in some of their writings the same philosophy of man that the European humanists had preached on the eve of the Renaissance.

Man's Autonomy

Inevitably, the naturalistic bent of Christian intellectualism conveyed not only the findings and affirmations of modern science, but

[23] For a typical direct attack, see *ibid.*, pp. 284–88; also see Shumayyil's open letter to Zaydan (*al-Hilal,* 1909) in which he questions Zaydan's religious argument of faith (*Mukhtarat,* vol. II, pp. 176–78).

[24] Antun, *Muqtatafat,* pp. 132–33.

above all the capacity to see the same thing from different points of view. Here was the root of relativism. But this trend developed only very gradually and took more than one generation to reach any kind of methodological self-consciousness. Formal categories, though they take longer to crystallize, tend to outlive the spontaneous attitudes which had given them rise; they are formed with minimal analysis, and therefore take longer to become part of the mental outlook.

At this stage the significance of the scientific approach lay mostly in another direction—a direction that affected the quality of consciousness. This "qualitative" change expressed itself in certain definite positions taken by some of the Christian writers. It is probably most clearly seen in the attempt to outline a rational theodicy. Under the impact of naturalism, interest shifted from analyzing the meaning of divine will to manipulating it in favor of practical ends. This shift was mirrored in the urgency with which scientific knowledge was acquired and organized; old conceptions were not refuted but prescinded. In an indirect way, the bases of old conceptions were shown to founder in the light of new laws—"the natural laws which govern all being, both animate and inanimate."[25]

The world, unmasked by science, now afforded the possibility of new cures; it afforded the opportunity for fulfillment and happiness. Fulfillment was no longer measured by conformity to "mystical precepts," but by action directed toward rationally recognized goals. In short, conduct was set against a new valuational frame of reference.

Antun suggested this revolutionary notion:[26] "Humanity alone is eternal," replacing, as Comte had done, the idea of divinity with that of humanity. Not only was a religious absolute overthrown in favor of a secular one, but also man's relationship to the absolute was transformed. Man found his fulfillment and happiness in relation to a concrete reality in which all men participated. "The more intense his participation the clearer and more perfect his happiness." Antun carried the humanization of social reality further by employing Emile Durkheim's idea of "collective consciousness." In defining collective consciousness as an expression or a reflection of man's collective intelligence and will, he provided the psychological grounds on which the transition from a God-oriented to a man-oriented mentality could be effected.

Antun drew attention to another interesting point. He distinguished between a popular (mass) mentality and an elite (khassah) mentality. The old nonscientific way of thought characteristic of the tradi-

[25] *Ibid.,* p. 128.   [26] *Ibid.,* p. 135.

tional generation he identified with the former; the modern scientific way of thought characteristic of modern Europe he identified with the latter. He was uncompromising in his refusal to admit religion's greatest consolation. "For the individual death is the end of everything; the popular belief in a life after death is meaningless and absurd."[27]

Likewise, Shumayyil eliminated the supernatural from the social outlook. Society, he maintained, is like nature, governed by rationally definable laws, and any reference to supernatural governance is simply misleading. Man in his social life is both autonomous and responsible. The laws regulating his social and political life are of his own making, the product of his "practical" reason. Shumayyil came close to the idea of natural law, dissociated from any specifically religious overtone and grounded solely in man's rationality. Man creates the law and designs it to suit his ends; laws are "changeable not fixed, limited not absolute."[28]

Shumayyil elaborated two other points of equal significance.[29] He set up as the primary criterion of the "just" law no other authority than that residing in "the mutual interest of men." In this he established the utilitarian principle at the center of political thought. He was also aware of the danger of arbitrariness. He declared that the truly civilized society can neither tolerate tyranny nor submit to arbitrary decree. Every society and every generation has its own distinctive requirements to which it should adjust its laws and legal structure. This adaptability he set up as the primary condition for social progress. Linking practical interest with scientific reasoning he eloquently demonstrated the inadequacy of the old ways in coping with new problems.

Postulates of Social Thought

Christian consciousness grounded itself in categories of thought that grew progressively more different from those employed by the Muslim writers of reformism. By the beginning of the twentieth century the two currents of thought, the Islamic reformist and the Christian westernizing, represented the two dominant intellectual currents in Egypt and the Fertile Crescent. The first posited rejuvenated Islam as the efficient engine for political and social reform, and the other felt that such reform would come with modernization based on

[27] *Ibid.*
[28] Shibli Shumayyil, "al-Ijtima' al-bashari w'al-'umran" [Society and Culture], *al-Muqtataf*, vol. IX (1885), p. 525.
[29] *Ibid.*, p. 524–25.

rationalism and science. The two movements took various forms, expressing themselves differently depending on the conditions. Also they influenced one another. But there is little doubt as to which one was endowed with resilience, vigor, and the capacity to grow. The retreat of Islamic reformism thus began early in the twentieth century; by mid-century it had all but collapsed.

Christian social thinking revolved around a few basic concepts, which formed its central guiding force. Let us define these concepts and briefly outline their significance.

The concept of change. The Christians believed that a tremendous force was at work transforming man and the world. They saw this change in moral terms. Thus Antun described it in terms of the materialistic orientation of modern society. He felt that materialism was "extending over the whole world," causing a situation where "old principles are undermined, laws uprooted, religion and morality destroyed."[30] True, Christian intellectuals often joined Muslim apologists in condemning the "merciless materialism of the West" and in contrasting it with the benign "spirituality of the East."[31] But the Christians, unlike the Muslims, were not blinded to the impossibility of reversing the trend or to the intrinsic desirability of change. In Christian intellectualism change was postulated as both fact and value.

Conflict. Another basic concept in Christian thinking was that the blind will working through nature manifests itself in man's relation to man. Thus it appeared inescapable that "men should fight and struggle and devour one another." "In society the big eat the small, the strong devour the weak, just as do the fish."[32] For the Christian intellectuals this echoed a truth not far from their own experience and situation, and they readily accepted its Darwinist formulation.

The idea of conflict within society replaced the idea of an external ordering of society. Absolute principles of order and justice were irrelevant to the concrete situation of social existence. Power and cunning, not values and principles, decided the fate of individuals and groups.

The same law determined relations among nations. "Nations face one another in enmity and hatred . . . and fight one another more mercilessly than wolves."[33] The decisive factor in political existence is

[30] Antun, *Muqtatafat,* p. 221.
[31] Amin Rihani (d. 1940) elaborated this contrast into a major theme in his political works.
[32] Antun, *Muqtatafat,* pp. 221–22.
[33] *Ibid.*

not the common bond of humanity but the will of the strong and their ability to impose it.

In Christian writings, this blind will is seen as fashioning the principles of human behavior. The idea of transcendental will determining the fate of societies and men was discarded. It was also implied that, given the concrete situation, both the scope and modality of political action were limited. Christian political thinking, as it became more and more realistic, became less and less optimistic regarding social reform.

Religion and society. The Christians believed that only through science, not religion, could social progress be made: "To say that by uniting around the banner of religion the Muslim nations could attain the same cultural level as the West (which has achieved it by scientific progress), is simply to ignore the way civilizations develop and to fail to understand human nature."[34] Only proper understanding of history and of what motivates human action could lead to a valid theory of society and of the methods of reforming it. Such understanding could be derived only from science; religious thought would only confuse the issue. Setting up religious unity (as Afghani had done) as the basis of social progress led only to "increasing weakness and dissolution . . . to retrogression and backwardness."[35]

The stress on this point increased as the spirit of nationalism spread. Christian writers became increasingly more open in their criticism of religiously oriented movements. Such movements were considered not only retrogressive but also exclusive as far as Christians and other non-Muslim Arab minorities were concerned. Its insistence on the secular foundations of history and society now began to acquire the character and tenacity of ideology.

Ideology. Christian intellectualism, however opposed to religious revivalist theory, could not blind itself to the efficacy of religious sentiment as an ideological force. As far as political utility was concerned, pan-Islamism was evidently of great importance. Distinction was thus made between ideological and purely religious values. Hence in resisting European imperialism the religious spirit was assigned a special role. As Antun put it, "There is a sense in which Pan-Islamism can be of great benefit as an instrument of resistance . . . ," but "the religious principle should not have unqualified primacy."[36] Its political value stopped where its ideological usefulness ended.

Christian political thought proceeded from another point: the need

[34] *Ibid.*, p. 151.   [35] *Ibid.*   [36] *Ibid.*

to protect religion itself. Paradoxically, it declared that it is not in the interest of religion to be the instrument of politics. The political manipulation of religion leads to the progressive drying up of the sources of faith and spiritual vitality. From this argument grew the need for the separation of church and state. Only within the framework of such a separation could the religious spirit be politically useful and at the same time safe from the corroding influences of sublunary motives.

In a series of articles in *al-Jami'a*,[37] Antun pinpointed a number of issues that other Christian writers had treated only peripherally. He criticized the "nonscientific character" of Afghani's and 'Abdu's political ideas and described their "idealistic position" as impractical.[38] Though he agreed with them that reform was necessary in the religious realm, he argued that in order to accomplish this reform the secular realm must be subjected to a different kind of reform. He accused them of having failed to make this essential distinction and, as a result, to have been guilty of contradiction.

Scientific realism required that reform in both the religious and secular spheres go hand in hand. In the religious realm the spirit of revelation would be restored and thus influence the conduct of man in society. But for "a new and vigorous humanity" to be created, "poverty, injustice and ignorance" must be overcome and "total social transformation" would be necessary. But to achieve this goal "political not religious reform" must have primacy.[39]

The Notions of Socialism

In the Arab world political consciousness received its earliest and most coherent formulations in the writings of the Christian avantgarde. Mainly as a result of their rational orientation and mode of life, they were driven to raise questions concerning economic and political conditions which their fellow Muslims were not in the position to raise. Because they were unencumbered with the kind of preconceptions that severely limited the scope of the Islamic reformists, the Christians enjoyed a definite advantage in their search for answers. Islamic revivalism, which provided the framework for all reformist thought, set definite limits even to the questions that were to be raised and prescribed the manner in which they were to be

---

[37] Particularly vol. V (1906).

[38] He showed great respect for 'Abdu. Of Afghani he spoke kindly but condescendingly: "He lived for intellectual things and was confined to the [impractical] world of ideas—like all enthusiastic idealists." *Ibid.*, p. 156.

[39] *Ibid.*, p. 157.

answered. Hence it was capable of making only the broadest generalizations regarding the empirical situation; it could never make concrete or specific definitions. Consequently, in the face of political reality reformism addressed itself not to the complexity of experienced social reality, but to an abstract realm of impotent dogmatic imperatives. Islamic reformism succeeded perhaps in reasserting Islamic dogma and building upon it an ideology of revivalism, but it failed in elaborating a coherent social outlook.

Some of the spokesmen for Muslim secularism adhered to a frame of reference which in a similar manner, though to a lesser extent, tended to restrict its field of vision. For a long time the dominant political principle animating Muslim secular consciousness was essentially negative: resistance to foreign incursion and domination. Nevertheless, within the national movement of Muslim secularism there were potentialities for doctrinal change and for a fresh social and political awareness that were lacking in Islamic reformism. Thanks mostly to the energizing influence of Christian political teaching these potentialities bore fruit, particularly in the development of a nationalist ideology.

Social detachment afforded the Christian intellectuals perspectives which neither the Islamic reformists nor the Muslim secularists enjoyed. The Muslims accepted their social and political situation as given, which provided them with a neutral background against which they raised their theoretical questions. But it did not take long before relevance between the theoretical formulations and the concrete social conditions was established. This process—of relating social thought to social reality—was achieved by the rebellious Christian vanguard with growing sharpness in the decade or so preceding World War I. A strong moral tone dominated this process. It can perhaps be said that the first coherent "left" in Arab thought was formed within its framework. From its assertions first arose the elements making for the evolution of genuine social consciousness in Arab society.

It is hard to trace the development of this "leftist" tendency in Arab Christian thought precisely because it was intertwined with so many other elements. It can perhaps be best indicated in terms of the principal stages of thought, which may be seen in three levels: the level of formal definition, the analytical, descriptive level, and the level of political commitment.

The first stage of Christian political consciousness was devoted to definitions, and it is best exemplified by Adib Ishaq and Butrus Bustani. On this level political consciousness responded not to immediate concerns but to an intellectual curiosity. The guiding interest was formal and abstract, a desire to define ideas and relations somewhat independently of the concrete situation. Ishaq, for example, defined government not in terms of its concrete political reality, but in terms of its formal structures and relationships.[40] The object of inquiry was simply to set forth general principles.[41] In Ishaq's writings we note the first moral formulations; however, they still remained on an abstract plane. The science of politics, though deriving from rational principles, was nevertheless intimately concerned with the problem of "virtue." According to Ishaq, laws in themselves are inefficient; they need a moral base to make them effective. "Political life, to be sound, must be founded on liberty; but liberty cannot be acquired except on the basis of virtue [fadila]."[42]

Bustani adopted a formal historical approach. In his encyclopedia, he stressed the historical evolution of various European political doctrines and creeds. In volume nine we have what is probably the first systematic exposition of socialist doctrine in the Arabic language. Bustani objectively analyzed the "materialistic teachings" of socialism, and, in a descriptive manner, he showed how these teachings, "already [1887] widespread in Russia and Western Europe," derived from various intellectual sources. Fichte, Fourier, Saint-Simon, Owen, Proudhon, and Büchner were singled out as the leading figures of materialistic socialism.[43]

On this formal level Christian thought showed much interest in the new science of "political economy." The first Arabic work on political economy was probably the book by Khalil Ghanim published in Alexandria in 1879.[44] The Principles of Political Economy, also written by a Christian, appeared in Cairo a decade later.[45] In the early

[40] Thus, "government is either despotic or consultative. Consultative government is either republican or monarchical," etc. Ishaq, "al-Mulk w'al-ra'iyya" [Sovereignty and Subjects], Majali, ed. Sufayr, p. 95. The switch to a higher level of analysis is illustrated by Shumayyil's definition, which related this abstract formulation to the concrete social situation: consultative government becomes "the highest form of government that man is capable of achieving. . . . limited monarchy is probably the best form of government for most nations." al-Muqtataf, vol. IX (1885), p. 528.

[41] E.g., "all forms of government are not applicable to all countries, nor are certain countries suited to certain forms . . ." Ishaq, "al-Mulk," Majali, ed. Sufayr, p. 95.

[42] Adib Ishaq, "al-Siyasa w'al-akhlaq" [Politics and Ethics], Majali, ed. Sufayr, p. 108.

[43] In Russia, Bustani points out, materialistic socialism expressed itself in nihilism: "The followers of this school of thought are called nihilists, which means the 'destroyers'; those who believe in nothing. Among their leaders were Chernyshevsky and Dobrolinov." Da'irat al-ma'arif, vol. IX (1887). Zaydan compared Russian nihilism to the Kharijites of Islam; see Mukhtarat, vol. II, p. 94; also al-Hilal, vol. VI (1897), pp. 293–94.

[44] Kitab al-iqtisad al-siyasi [The Book of Political Economy].

[45] Rafla Jirjis, Usul al-iqtisad al-siyasi (Cairo, 1886).

1890s, economic problems began to be discussed in the Lebanese periodical press.[46]

But systematic analysis crystallized on the second level—the analytical, descriptive phase—which was reached after the turn of the century. This level of political consciousness is best exemplified in some of the writings of Sarruf and Zaydan.

It is possible that Sarruf might have been influenced by certain socialist ideas current in Europe at the end of the nineteenth century. This can be seen in his novel, *Fatat misr* [Egypt's Daughter], in which war and imperialism are attributed to European capitalism—"big business, industry, and capital."[47] Sarruf, however, generally upheld an essentially liberal position and favored the evolutionary rather than the revolutionary approach to social and political problems.

It was from Zaydan, who wrote a series of articles on the subject, that the doctrine of socialism received a comprehensive analysis. In his formulation of the basic conceptions of the socialist doctrine he reflected the attitude of enlightened middle class Christians. He defined socialism in terms of two main values: justice and progress. Socialist doctrine, according to Zaydan, portrayed bourgeois society as suffering from a political and economic "imbalance." Injustice was the product of this lack of equilibrium, because "wealth and social privilege" were the monopoly of the few. Socialism called for supporting the weak and the poor against the strong and the rich. "In this [call]," Zaydan observed, "socialism is as old as human society itself." Since the principle of progress made change an imperative of social action, socialists were backed not only by a moral imperative but also by the scientific principle of evolution. For Zaydan evolution represented betterment in "all conditions of life"; it led to systematic reform aiming at the removal of injustice in society.[48]

Zaydan attributed the distinctively "communist type" of socialism to "Marx and his followers." He treated Marxism briefly and superficially, and singled out the concept of surplus value as the central idea in Marxism: "The fundamental basis of Marx's theory is that the difference between what the capitalist pays as wages—an amount just enough to keep the worker and his family alive—and the price for

---

[46] See, for example, 'Isa Iskander al-Ma'luf's (d. 1956) analysis of the meaning of economics: "al-Iqtisad," *Lubnan* (1892). Economics or political economy is defined as "the science concerned with capital accumulation . . ." Text in *Ishaq*, "al-Siyasa," *Majali*, ed. Sufayr, pp. 148ff.

[47] Sarruf, *Fatat misr*, p. 76.

[48] Zaydan, *Mukhtarat*, vol. II, pp. 85–86, 92. In making the distinction between socialism and communism, he had three "utopian" socialists in mind: Saint-Simon (pp. 88–89), Fourier (pp. 89–90), and Owen (pp. 90–91),

which he sells the product of labor is acquired by the capitalist [as profit]."[49]

For both Zaydan and Sarruf, socialism was not an unmitigated evil (Zaydan wrote admiringly of Fabianism).[50] It served to draw attention to the ills of modern society and thus to contribute to curing them. But they regarded socialist doctrines as untenable both in terms of their philosophic validity and their social feasibility. In the first place, they regarded complete equality among men as impossible: men are inherently unequal, they "differed in their talents and in their capabilities."[51] This was taken to be so self-evident that neither writer thought it necessary to elaborate further on the subject. Both assumed that there existed important differences not only between individuals but also between classes and religious or ethnic groups. Both Sarruf and Zaydan looked down on the "masses."

Society was seen as hierarchical both in its evolution and its structure. In the works of both Sarruf and Zaydan there was an implicit acceptance of the social and economic "inequalities" which socialism sought to eliminate. They found it in the nature of things that real power rested not with the mass of the people but with the elite (*khassah*)—an aristocracy which played the role of ward (*wasi*) in society.[52] Political struggle was essentially an internal struggle between cliques within the ruling class; the masses were instruments in the political struggle.[53] It was not political or social doctrine nor the form of government that was the determining factor in distributing power and wealth; rather, it was the power struggle.

Another consideration posed by socialist theory was how control was to be taken over in society. Zaydan regarded the economic aspect as more important than the political. He saw insurmountable barriers in the way of an economic take-over by the government. He was convinced that if socialism were ever to succeed it would be through evolutionary reform. He dismissed the Marxist doctrine of the inevitability of class struggle and ruled out the necessity of the collapse of the capitalistic system from within. Even if the state succeeded in gaining control over economic life the central problem would still remain. For the elimination of competition and the destruction of the free market economy would lead to an economic breakdown. Thus socialism, though morally justified, was impossible to realize for pragmatic reasons: "In many of its aspects it [socialism] is right, but realizing it in practice is impossible or nearly impossible."[54]

[49] *Ibid.*, pp. 92–93.   [50] *Ibid.*, p. 99.   [51] *Ibid.*, pp. 97–98.
[52] The members of this elite were the ones who "wielded real sovereignty . . . who legislated and set down the rules." *Ibid.*, p. 38.
[53] "The masses only imagine that they act freely." *Ibid.*, p. 38.
[54] *Ibid.*, p. 103.

In 1913, after a sojourn in western Europe, Zaydan added a significant observation.[55] He said that when socialism first made its appearance in Europe as a political movement it had "aimed at replacing the existing order"; but that with the passage of time it had become absorbed into parliamentary political parties and undergone profound change. It no longer aimed at undermining the established order but rather only "at reforming what has become corrupted in it." Socalism has become an accepted reformist movement, just as he had thought it ought to be.

The third level, that of political commitment, was dominated by Shumayyil and Antun, the Christian romantic radicals par excellence. In their writings they represent the starting point of a progressive left in contemporary Arab thought. They differed from other Christian writers in two basic respects. First, they dealt with the social problem comprehensively and established a relatively thorough and closely reasoned position with regard to social action. Second, they assumed a position of passionate ideological commitment.

From their standpoint, social injustice and economic inequality were the product not merely of social evolution, but rather of conflict within society. They attributed the cause of conflict directly to the competitive economic system characteristic of capitalism. Antun declared: "The conflict we see in the world today has one cause, the lack of [government] control over business, industry and labor."[56] Both Antun and Shumayyil drifted away from the libertarian position typical of most of the educated Christian Arabs and assigned to the state the task of correcting society's injustices. This was to follow the reform of the state itself, which under bourgeois conditions was the instrument of the ruling minority and had "but one function, to protect individuals and safeguard the existing order."[57]

Antun's drift to the left seemed to have gained momentum, oddly enough, after his arrival in the United States in 1904. In New York al-Jami'a increasingly turned to the analysis of social and economic problems. During this period, Antun's collaborator was an obscure Christian writer of Lebanese origin who wrote some of the best analytical articles in al-Jami'a.[58]

[55] Jurji Zaydan, "Nizam al-ijtima' wa hal yumkin qalbuhu" [The Social Order: Can It Be Overthrown?], Mukhtarat, vol. II, p. 46.
[56] "Muhammad 'Abdu wa ara'uhu fi l-mushkila al-ijtima-'iyya" [Muhammad 'Abdu and His Views Concerning the Social Problem], al-Jami'a, vol. V (1904), p. 177.
[57] Ibid.
[58] Niqula Haddad (d. 1954). See, for example, his analysis of the ills of the American social system: "First, the present system encourages the concentra-

Both Shumayyil and Antun saw in socialism not merely the promise of future reform but the only salvation of man and society. Like Zaydan, they regarded the development of socialistic sensibility as concomitant with social evolution. But for Shumayyil, and also for Antun, the socialist view was not "just another doctrine, but an intrinsic part of man's attitude toward the social order. [Socialist ideas] are inherent in the teachings of all philosophers and all reformers throughout the ages."[59] Shumayyil, who was fairly well-read in socialist literature, laid great emphasis on the distinction between *ishtirakiyya*—"the misleading Arabic translation of the French word *socialisme*"—and *ijtima'iyya*—the correct translation. His intention was to make clear that "socialism" meant something quite different from the Arabic word *ishtirakiyya* (association; v. *ishtaraka,* to join, to become associated with), and to relate it to its etymological origin, *ijtima'* (society, community). "The term 'Socialism' is derived from the word 'society' [mujtama'], which derives from the word 'culture' or 'civilization' ['umran]." As a doctrine, socialism did not call for absolute equality, but simply for "a fair sharing of benefits between labor and capital." In the last analysis all that socialism aimed at was "to provide man with the means to achieve happiness on earth, to restore his lost paradise."[60]

In Shumayyil and Antun there emerges for the first time in Arab thought an awareness of the common man, of the vast impoverished strata of Arab society. And for the first time the masses are not looked down upon; they are the center of concern. What did socialism aim at achieving for the common man?

> . . . reducing his misery; assuring him his minimum needs and protecting his rights . . . lifting him up and raising him to the level of human beings; teaching him to have his rightful place in society [and] assuring him his just share of the social product.[61]

For Antun the main problem was not one of defining the meaning and goals of socialism as it was of bringing about the socialist order.[62]

---

tion of business in the hands of a few who control it. . . . Secondly, although America's wealth is great, it is unfairly distributed among the producers. Greed and deception determine distribution. This unfair distribution is America's greatest misfortune; it is worse in America than in any other country in the world." *al-Jami'a,* vol. VI (1908), p. 117.

[59] *Majmu'a,* vol. II, p. 153. Originally published in the Cairo daily *al-Akhbar* in 1908.

[60] *Ibid.,* pp. 153–54.

[61] "And the distribution of benefits," Shumayyil added, "will be in accordance with work accomplished." *Ibid.,* p. 153. This was probably taken from Enfantin's and Basard's famous dictum: "A chacun selon sa capacité, à chaque capacité selon ses oeuvres."

[62] Antun, *Mulhaq majallat al-sayyidat w'al-rijal* (Cairo, 1923), p. 30.

Antun was, if not for outright revolution, at least for vigorous action, which did not exclude violence. He was convinced that it was not enough "to preach socialism if one wished to bring it about." He held that it was probably necessary to establish socialism by force, and therefore it was also necessary to implant the idea of violence in the minds of the young. Otherwise socialism would "forever remain just a theory."[63] He formulated the motto: "Learn, but above all learn how to act."[64]

Antun lived long enough to see the outbreak of the Bolshevik revolution which he passionately hailed. Like George Sorel, he was fearful that it might fail because it broke out in Russia rather than in a West European country: he doubted whether the Russian people were "able to carry out the great transformation." He believed, also like Sorel, that if the revolution failed in Russia the "Socialist movement would be checked in every other country in the world."[65] But when he died in 1922 he was confident that a socialist state had been firmly established in the world.

[63] *Ibid.*, p. 131.
[64] "*I'malu la i'lamu faqat.*"
[65] Antun, *Mulhaq*, pp. 14, 131.

Chapter VI

The Emergence of Muslim Secularism

Who precisely were the Muslim secularists? What were the common elements that gave them a distinct identity? Of the Arab intellectuals this group is perhaps the most difficult to define.

The term "Muslim secularist" derives from the fact that this group
of Arab intellectuals was Muslim (hence to be differentiated from the
Christian westernizing intellectuals) and that they were not religiously oriented (hence to be differentiated from the Muslim traditionalists and reformists). By the same token, they shared characteristics with these other groups. Their tendency to venture beyond the
religious frame of reference and to appeal to secular values and
norms, especially with regard to politics, gave them a common ground
with the Christian westernizing intellectuals. But they also had an
Islamic mental outlook. For the Muslim secularist identification with
Islam (as well as with its characteristic mode of thought) went
beyond the purely conscious and rational. In this respect no matter
how strong the unity in will and outlook achieved between Muslim
secularism and Christian intellectualism, the Islamic element inherent
in Muslim secularism always set strict limits to this unity.

For the educated Muslim generation the psychological significance
of Islam was qualitatively different from what Christianity was for the
Christian intellectuals. While for the Christian intellectuals a more or
less complete break (at least as far as rational outlook was concerned) with religious assumptions was possible, for the Muslim
secularists the process of secularization stopped at the borderline of
inherited dogma and thus remained essentially qualified. Muslim
secularism, then, though intimately connected with both an Islamic
and a secular position, maintained a more or less independent
perspective. In certain extreme situations it expressed itself in typical
Islamic reformist terms and was identifiable with Islamic reformism.
Frequently, however, when it carried the banner of rebellion, it
upheld the cause of secularism and innovation.

Islam and secularism were thus the two main characteristics of
what we have labeled the Muslim secularist intellectuals. The position
of this group represented the focal point of intellectual polarity of this

period, and, as a result, this position lacked sharp doctrinal focus. The Muslim secularist generation tended to move away from theories and toward the more immediate and the concrete. Earlier, we characterized this polarity in terms of dialectical interplay between two related positions.[1] This dialectical relationship, however, should not be overemphasized: Muslim secularism, even as an incomplete synthesis of Islamic reformist and Christian westernizing intellectualism, became the dominant outlook of the ruling national bourgeoisie in the subsequent (interwar) period.

Social Composition

The Muslim secularist intellectuals of this period belonged to the first post-traditional generation of Muslims to appear in the modern Arab world.[2] In the Fertile Crescent practically all the leading members of this group came from the upper and middle classes and belonged to established urban families (of Basra and Baghdad, Aleppo and Damascus, Beirut and Jerusalem). In Egypt its social background was somewhat different; many of its members had middle class and humble rural origins.

In Syria and Iràq the Muslim secularist generation came to the fore about the turn of the century, and it began assuming a leading role in social and political life after the Young Turk coup d'etat of 1908. In Egypt, though the formative influences date back to the 1870s and the 'Urabi movement, the emergence of this group as a politically active force began in the middle 1890s with the crystallization of nationalist resistance under Mustafa Kamel (1874–1908).

This group was composed of various elements. There were, first, the politicians and administrative officials of the Egyptian and Ottoman civil service bureaucracies; they usually belonged to the rich or influential Sunni families. Second, there were the professionals, particularly lawyers and doctors. Many members of this category abandoned their professional careers in favor of politics, literature, or journalism. Third, there were the *hommes de lettres,* the journalists and essayists who with the written word exercised considerable influ-

---

[1] See Chapter I.

[2] Those studied here belong to two categories: writers and political activists. There were, of course, writers who were politically active and activists who occasionally wrote. Among those whose writings and/or political activities influenced political attitude and thought, and who are studied here, are: Qasim Amin (1863–1908), 'Abdul-Rahman al-Kawakibi (1849–1902), Waliyy al-Din Yakan (1873–1921), Muhammad Kurd 'Ali (1876–1953), Shakib Arslan (1869–1945), Rafiq al-'Azm (1865–1924), Ahmad Lutfi al-Sayyid (1872–1963), Muhammad Husayn Haykal (1888–1956), Ma'ruf al-Rusafi (1875–1945), Sidqi al-Zahawi (1863–1936).

ence on political development. Fourth, there was the separate group of army officers, who were particularly important in Syria and Iraq. (In terms of direct political action, this group constituted the vanguard of the nationalist movement; it was the backbone of the "secret societies" between 1908 and 1914, and it played a significant role in the Arab revolt of 1916.) Finally, there was the student group, the young Muslims studying in Constantinople, Paris, and elsewhere in the Middle East or Europe, who constituted the rising militant intellectuals of Arab nationalism.

Social Experience and Education

From the sociological as well as from the corresponding psychological point of view, the Muslim secularists belonged to a world rather different from that to which Christian intellectuals were accustomed. As we have seen, the typical young Muslim intellectual, whether Egyptian, Syrian, or Iraqi, was born into a world to which he felt unquestioning belonging. He experienced none of the tensions or feelings of alienation to which his Christian counterpart was exposed: There was no uprooting pull, no need to seek his future elsewhere; he instinctively felt that his destiny was bound to this world. The status quo provided him with all the necessary elements with which to shape his life. From his standpoint, even the negative political aspects of his society offered a positive value: Turkish oppression in the Fertile Crescent and British occupation in Egypt were challenges which sharpened his sense of identity and enhanced his feeling of belonging; his life had unity and purpose which were characteristically lacking in the life of the uprooted Christian. It is important to point out that intellectual rebellion for the Muslim secular intellectual was strictly a political experience, whereas for the typical Christian it represented a total existential experience.

This life, protected by the familiar and the securely possessed, provided the conditions for both economic and psychological self-sufficiency. As a child, the Muslim was socialized within the ambit of the traditional culture. At home and at school he was inculcated with all the values of his social class and religion. He was not exposed to a western-type education until adolescence or early manhood, which reduced its impact. His tastes, values, and preferences, as well as his basic psychological orientations had already congealed.

His higher education took him to Beirut, Cairo, Constantinople, or Europe (which to most young men of this generation meant Paris). Constantinople and Paris represented the outside world. But for the young Muslim from Baghdad or Cairo or Damascus, Paris belonged to a wholly foreign world, while Constantinople was still part of the familiar environment. In Constantinople he was exposed to basically the same culture and values that had governed his early life and upbringing. Even the language was familiar in most cases.

Ottoman education was primarily professional education. It provided training in three principal fields: law, medicine, and the military. It normally produced an "Ottomanized" Arab—one whose attitude and bearing were patterned after those of the "Europeanized" Turk. It is important to note that the westernization of a significant part of this Muslim generation was effected through the intermediary of Ottoman example and education rather than directly.

The experience of the Muslim Arab in Paris was rather different. Here his alienation from the environment was complete, a fact which greatly influenced his formal education and his reactions to the outside world. A large proportion of Muslim students studying in Paris during this period did not complete their course of study. This was owing in part to the many distractions that Paris offered, but mainly to inadequate previous academic training, especially in languages. The accomplishment of this Muslim Arab generation, as far as systematic study in Europe was concerned, appears to have been rather limited. It used to be a matter of pride for parents to say of their sons returning after a few years in Europe that they had not "changed" and were as true to "their traditions and customs" as when they left.[3] It was fairly easy for the young Muslim Arab not to "change"; his typical attitude toward Paris (and toward Europe generally) was first one of fear and hostility which later changed to one of affected haughtiness not unmixed with awe. His shyness, loneliness, and many frustrations tended to blind him to the strange society around him, and greatly restricted his capacity to learn and to benefit from his opportunity. Europe never appeared so distant as it did from the heart of Paris.

This is perhaps understandable, especially when we compare the situation of the Muslim with that of his Christian compatriot. The young Christian arriving in Paris in, say, 1910 felt as much at ease as did his fellow Muslim arriving in Constantinople, and for similar reasons. He was relatively fluent in French and could find his way

---

[3] There was resentment against those who came back Europeanized (*tafarnuj*), but many did not "Europeanize." "Many young men who studied in Europe have come back with their traditional customs and manners intact . . . To such young men the term *tafarnuj* cannot apply." al-Nadim, *Sulafah*, vol. I, p. 83.

around Paris without difficulty. It was not hard to adapt to the Parisian environment; indeed, it was more congenial and more enjoyable than the one he had known in Beirut, or Aleppo, or Cairo.

For this Muslim generation contact with Europe evoked a negative response. It made it nostalgic for its own traditional culture and values and hostile toward those of Europe. The young Muslim studying in Europe developed an anti-European attitude and took refuge in idealizing Islam and Islamic culture. This turning inward created barriers against proper understanding of the West, particularly its science and art. Only through literature, history, and politics did the young Muslim acquire some understanding of Europe's intellectual heritage. But the gulf was never completely bridged. The valuational principles and methodological considerations informing European knowledge and taste remained beyond his mental horizon.

Basic Intellectual Orientations

The mental outlook characteristic of Muslim secularism best expressed itself in terms of the two formative forces to which it was most exposed: Islamic reformism and Christian westernizing intellectualism. As a movement of thought it was made up of a propensity for modernization and, at the same time, a tendency toward fundamental reformism.

Christian intellectualism exerted its decisive influence on Muslim secularism as the intermediary of modern ideas. The style of modern thought was conveyed by Bustani and Zaydan, Sarruf and Shumayyil, Haddad and Antun. Through them an understanding of Europe was made possible on a different level, and it was achieved in Arabic. They were responsible for making basic modernizing attitudes acceptable. Somehow the glint of novelty was rendered less obvious by the Arabic terminology, and the revolutionary edge of innovating ideas less cutting by its familiar imagery.

Muslim secularists operated at a level that concealed contradictions which were not to become obvious until the next generation. In their intellectual efforts they tended to follow the course of least resistance. Impatient with philosophical subtleties, they increasingly tended toward preoccupation with practical interests. In its ideological formulations Muslim secularism sought its most reliable grounds not in the religious utopianism of the Islamic reformists (to which, however, much lip service was rendered), nor in the rationalistic pragmatism of the Christian intellectuals, but in politics.

From the point of view of nationalism the decisive factor was Europe. Like the Christian intellectuals, the Muslim secularists recognized Europe as the main agent of modernization;[4] but, like the Islamic reformists, they also regarded it as the major political threat. The former attitude provided the basis for the modernizing impetus, the latter for the stress on Islamic rejuvenation and reform. But before analyzing these attitudes, let us briefly examine the representative position of Qasim Amin (d. 1908), probably the leading Muslim secularist intellectual of this period, in whose works secularism achieved its highest expressions.

Qasim Amin and Secularist Positivism

The world of Qasim Amin was the world of the Christian intellectuals, of rationalist and western-oriented thought, of the advocates of modernization. Amin was the forerunner of the westernized Muslim Arab of the mid-twentieth century. He provided the first systematic formulations of Muslim secularism, expressed not abstractly but in terms of the concrete social problems of the day.[5]

Amin was a contemporary of Muhammad 'Abdu and on friendly terms with him. Yet the fundamental premises forming his intellectual position were in many ways directly opposed to 'Abdu's. Amin's and 'Abdu's lifetimes came at the center of the period of the Awakening, and they represent perhaps the most profound intellectual cleavage within modern Islam. But their opposition, never carried out to its limit in frank confrontation, remained latent. This was characteristic of Muslim secularism, which failed to fulfill its critical task with respect to Islamic reformism.

What fundamentally distinguished Amin's position was its uncompromising adherence to positivistic starting points. The religious problem was thus viewed primarily through its social aspects. Religion's metaphysical assertions as such were not questioned; they were simply relegated to an extrascientific realm, where they lost their social relevance. While 'Abdu invoked the principle of rationality to bolster a doctrine of religious revival, Amin invoked it for purposes tending in the opposite direction. Reason for Amin signified science,

---

[4] "An obvious truth, which we are not the first to declare, is that our awakening is due to the impact of modern European civilization." al-Mu'tamar al-'arabi al-awwal [Proceedings of the First Arab Conference] (Cairo, 1913), p. 21.

[5] Amin's two major works, Tahrir al-mar'ah [Liberation of Women] (Cairo, 1899) and al-Mar'a al-jadidah [The New Woman] (Cairo, 1901), are devoted to the problem of the status of women in Muslim society. This problem was first taken up half a century earlier by Butrus al-Bustani; see "Ta'lim al-nisa'" [Education of Women] (1849), al-Rawa'i', ed. Fu'ad Afram al-Bustani (Beirut, 1929), pp. 24ff. Both writers believed that women should be educated, given their rights, and raised to a moral and legal status equal to that of men.

and science in its application to society's ills provided its own values and cures.

Still, there were certain elements common to both positions. Above all, they both had to confront more or less the same problems, and their recourse to "reason and logic" signified a common intellectual universe. Also 'Abdu, unlike the conservative *ulema,* who impugned the very foundations of science, sought to establish a ground on which science could somehow be reconciled with religion (or vice versa). Amin, for his part, established the primacy of positive science without attacking religious authority, and treated religion with seemingly genuine respect. Of course, in the two positions there were clearly discernible fundamental premises which on closer examination were seen to be simply irreconcilable.

Amin's peculiar kind of positivism as it related to the central social problems will clarify the basic differences. His social analysis took a typically social Darwinist tone—the primacy of conflict in all social relations.[6] He pushed aside the moralistic attitudes of Islamic reform- ism and declared society's survival to depend not on morality or religion but on the "fitness to take part in struggle."[7] Although Amin, like Shumayyil and Antun, inclined toward a naturalistic view of man and society, he did not allow himself to be drawn into a position of philosophical materialism. It was never sufficient, he declared, merely to possess material power. For just as formal ethical or religious principles alone never provided the conditions for real power, mate- rial means had their effectiveness in something other than the mere force which they discharged. He strove to lay positive foundations for a "new mentality" which partook of "reason and science, the basis of all power."[8] He had no fear of competing with Europe. "If a nation keeps up with the knowledge possessed by its competitors . . . it will be able to compete with them, [even] overtake them."[9]

In his introduction to *al-Mar'a al-jadidah,* Amin stated that science was the only valid foundation of truth, and utility the only valid test of value. In this he was at one with the Tunisian Khayr al-Din, the first Muslim secularist to defend the utilitarian approach in dealing with the social issue. Amin and Khayr al-Din were exposed to the same French influences, particularly to Comtean positivist philoso- phy. Amin in addition was much impressed by Herbert Spencer.

---

[6] Amin, *Tahrir,* p. 94.   [7] *Ibid.,* p. 95.

[8] *Ibid.* Alfred North Whitehead has also pointed out: "The new mentality is more important even than the new science or the new technology." *Science and the Modern World,* Signet ed. (New York, 1962), p. 10.

[9] Amin, *Tahrir,* p. 95.

Like all nineteenth-century positivists, Amin was convinced that the key to the salvation of Muslim society was in overcoming ignorance and in spreading knowledge and enlightenment. In this respect his secularist bias did not vary much from 'Abdu's reformist bias: They both believed that social problems would be resolved and conflicts reconciled if the truth—whether in the scientific or the religious sense—were brought to bear on them. Both positions were dominated by the same optimistic faith in reason. In both perspectives, man in his concrete empirical being and society in its secular or religious reality were the objects of the final and highest manifestations of good. However, from Amin's secular perspective, good was viewed in terms of a practical and material good rather than in terms of a "spiritual" or a moral state of being.

Amin, expressing a basic element of the rising bourgeoisie's ideology, gave lengthy and reasoned insistence on "individual freedom." Influenced by French liberalism, he was especially interested in freedom of speech and freedom of belief: "Real freedom consists in the individual's being able to express any opinion, to preach any creed, to propagate any doctrine."[10] Positing this basic freedom, he derived certain rights which were particularly important for a rising middle class—the right to demand change, to voice opposition. Nothing in society was above criticism, and any individual, basing his thoughts on reason and science, had the right to question custom, law, or education. He was probably the first Muslim intellectual to declare publicly: "In a truly free country no one should be afraid to renounce his fatherland, to repudiate belief in God and his prophets, or to impugn the laws and customs of his people."[11]

Amin was profoundly affected by the misery of the masses in Egypt. But in typical positivist fashion he attributed it to stubborn conservatism and blind resistance to change. "Among the causes of our suffering is the fact that we base our life on traditions which we no longer understand, which we preserve only because they have been handed down to us . . ."[12] He insisted that what was valuable in society was not "inherited tradition," but what best served the "social interest" (maslahat al-mujtama'): "We should cultivate those customs and habits that would best serve our social interest."[13] He tried neither to justify discarding age-old habits nor to give excuses for learning from the West. His moderate tone, not only his eloquent arguments, was responsible for the warm reception he received in reformist and secularist circles alike.

[10] Cited in Ahmad Khaki, Qasim Amin (Cairo, 1945), p. 48.
[11] Ibid.   [12] Amin, Tahrir, p. 154.   [13] Ibid.

History for Amin evoked neither religious reverence nor rationalist nostalgia. He took a cold view of the past: The past should not "be cast away altogether," but neither should it be swallowed whole. It should be "examined carefully and patiently so that the harmful elements in it may be separated from the beneficial."[14] History should be assessed not only in terms of its content but also in terms of its social usefulness.

Amin was among the few Muslims of his generation to view Islamic culture dispassionately and to take a critical attitude toward it. For example: "Muslims in all their history never attained the same level [of culture] as did the Greeks or the Romans, particularly in their [political] contribution. . . ."[15] He singled out Islam's shortcomings in developing legal and political institutions, and considered self-evident the superiority of modern Europe in this realm.[16]

Amin was convinced that society was "governed by continuous, imperceptible change." Four main forces determined this process of change: physical environment, heredity or ethnic background, social interaction, and scientific invention.[17] There was no absolute principle with which to measure or evaluate change. One thing was certain, however: what was good or useful for one society was not necessarily so for another.

Amin was a skeptic, but his philosophical and moral positions were set forth in such a way as to conceal his irreligious attitude. Values were relative; whether moral or aesthetic, they appeared and possessed meaning only in a social context and exerted pressure only in a social milieu. Value was real only in the attitude and actions of men. As such, values were inseparable from social existence, and social change necessarily brought change in value systems. Progress was not only material, it was also moral and aesthetic. Thus his often-repeated dictum: "Scientific progress leads to moral progress."[18]

If the past was something deficient and incomplete, the future was perfectable. 'Abdu's backward-looking position was reversed. But Amin in his uncompromising positivism never allowed himself to be alienated from his Muslim intellectual environment. He was a practical and prudent man. His attitude demonstrated the possibility of intellectual coexistence between Islamic reformism and Muslim secularism. In one sense he encouraged the advance of scientific rationalism, but in another he strengthened the habit of avoiding frontal

---

[14] *Ibid.,* p. 155. [15] Amin, *al-Mar'a,* pp. 177–78.
[16] *Ibid.,* p. 178. [17] Amin, *Tahrir,* p. 8.
[18] Amin, *al-Mar'a,* p. 201. Here he refers repeatedly to Spencer, see pp. 202–4.

confrontations with established belief. In his writings and in his social attitude, Amin embodied, as probably no other Muslim secularist has done, not only some of the highest achievements of Muslim secularism but also some of its most profound contradictions.

Muslim Secularism and the West

The most dazzling aspect of contemporary Europe was, from the Muslim secularist standpoint, its "modernity." And the essence of modernity resided in two elements: science and constitutional government. "If only two things were present, science and constitutional government," some commentators believed that progress and power would be within reach of Arab society.[19] But as to the structure and specific content of science and constitutional government, the secularist writers showed little interest.

The overriding passion of the Muslim secularists, in their relation to Europe, was not thought but action. They were primarily interested in bringing about a transformation of the prevailing condition of "weakness" and "backwardness." Change for them was exigent. This desire for immediate change reflected an attitude of mind rather than a reasoned principle of action; beyond the assertion of the need for reform there was little by way of defining the nature of that need or the method of fulfilling it: "no matter how much we disagree about reform, we all agree on the necessity of reform."[20]

What should be borrowed from the West? The answer offered by the Muslim secularists was not an analytical answer, but a slogan: Borrow that which is useful, discard that which is not.[21] The West was regarded as a storehouse of good and bad things. All that was needed was to reach out and select the good things prudently.

From the start Muslim secularism showed itself especially wary when it came to ideas. Curiously enough, religious considerations seemed secondary; the distinction between the secular and the religious spheres was made not in terms of dogma but in terms of practical interest.[22] The formula for borrowing the useful and reject-

---

[19] Rafiq al-'Azm (d. 1924), "al-Jami'ah al-islamiyyah wa uruba" [The Islamic Community and Europe], *Majmu'ah: Athar Rafiq bayk al-'Azm* [Collected Works of Rafiq al-'Azm], ed. 'Uthman al-'Azm (Cairo, 1925), p. 80.

[20] Rafiq al-'Azm, *al-Durus al-hikmiyyah lil-nashi'ah al-islamiyyah* [Wise Instructions to the Rising Muslim Generation] (Damascus, 1909), p. 3.

[21] This, however, was an attitude common to all nonwestern societies challenged by the West. E.g., in Meiji Japan, Shiba Shiro (d. 1885) advised ". . . taking from America what is useful and rejecting what is only superficial." See G. B. Sanson, *The Western World and Japan* (New York, 1949), p. 414.

[22] As Khayr al-Din had put it: "If a believer considers a man in the wrong in

ing the harmful was a practical device aimed more at accommodating innovation than at safeguarding tradition. In actual practice, two attitudes became generally prevalent, one which regarded everything western as basically "bad," and another which accepted the West's "superiority" without question.

Another dimension of the Muslim secularists' attitude toward the West was a strong feeling of inferiority. This derived not from military defeat inflicted at the hands of Europe nor from any sense of weakness. Indeed, the belief was common among the secularist writers that Islam, an imperial power from medieval times, was only temporarily in eclipse, and that its military resurgence may be at hand. The sense of inferiority came from another source deriving from Europe's own bearing. There was a mystery about European life and character. Europeans seemed to possess some kind of power which eluded explicit definition. They appeared capable of great good and great evil.[23] Greater familiarity with Europeans did nothing to dispel this feeling; it only confirmed and strengthened it.

It is easy to see how western society and intellectual tradition rarely came into full focus for the Muslim secularist. Muslim secularism, as a current of thought and as a political awareness, seemed unable to cope in a rational and consistent manner with the intellectual challenge presented by European civilization. The general response was rarely as constructive as that of Qasim Amin. The distinctive secularist style was declamatory; it cultivated a slogan-oriented, hyperbolical, and hortative attitude which dominated political life in the first half of the twentieth century.

For Islamic reformism the dominant force framing the relationship with the West was the idea of a resurrected Islam, and for Christian intellectualism it was the spirit of rational and scientific enlightenment. In Muslim secularist consciousness the idea of the West as a complete other attained its fullness. This is one reason why communication between the Muslim secularists and the West was always partial and inadequate.

As a social group, the Muslim secularists were probably the most directly affected by the onslaught of Europe. Their position forced

---

his religious belief, he will not for this reason hesitate to imitate him in his [good] *secular* habits." (Italics added.) *Muqaddimat kitab aqwam al-masalik fi ma'rifat ahwal al-mamalik* (Constantinople, 1876), p. 60.

[23] In his first novel, Muhammad Husayn Haykal observed: "Egyptians used to believe in the genius of [European] foreigners; they regarded them as either angels or devils. . . . They were convinced that these foreigners possessed a knowledge beyond our power to comprehend." *Hakatha khuliqtu* [I was Born Like This] (Cairo, 1909), p. 10.

them to politicize the most nonpolitical problems; every issue became power-oriented.

It must be remembered that the first political resistance to the West emerged from the ranks of Muslim secularism. The hostility of this generation of Muslims to the West is probably comparable only to that of the Japanese intellectuals of the early part of the nineteenth century.[24] Let us consider a few expressions of this attitude.

Ethnic differentiation. 'Abdul Rahman al-Kawakibi expressed anti-West sentiments in terms of innate ethnic characteristics:

> Western man is a hard-headed materialist. He is fierce to deal with, he is by nature inclined to exploit others, and is ever ready to revenge himself on his enemies. He has lost the last trace of feeling and charity which Christianity had bestowed upon him. The Teutonic (including Anglo-Saxon) German is naturally tough. He regards the weak with disdain, as unworthy of existing. He considers force man's highest virtue. Power for him derives from wealth: he loves science not for its own sake but because it makes him rich. He seeks glory in order to achieve wealth. As for the Latin, he is of mercurial character. Reason to him means overstepping limits; his life has little modesty in it; honor exhibits itself in gaudy apparel. Glory is won by bringing other people under his sway.
>
> [Arabs and eastern people in general are] morally motivated and are governed by kindness of heart, compassion and mercy, which they often misplace. They are gentle and kind even to their enemies.[25]

Cultural superiority. Western manners were considered to be inferior to those of the East. *Tafarnuj* (affecting European manners and dress) is regarded with distaste. 'Azma writes: "It is a great disaster that has befallen us . . . imitating Europeans thus. We must get rid of this sickly habit which has been not only financially ruinous to us but has also opened the doors for economic domination by Europe. It has helped the Europeans to achieve their [political] goals as well as to humiliate the people of the East."[26]

Western aggressiveness. Kawakibi developed the view that Europe-

---

[24] See Aziwa Seishisai's analysis in *New Proposals* (1825), text in *Sources of Japanese Tradition,* ed. Ryusaku Tsunodo, William Theodore de Bary, and Donald Keene (New York, 1958), pp. 602–3.

[25] 'Abdul-Rahman al-Kawakibi, *Taba'i' al-istibdad wa masari' al-isti'bad* [The Characteristics of Tyranny and the Crimes of Oppression] (Cairo, n.d.), p. 79. As for the English, Afghani gave this definition: "The Englishman has little intelligence but great perseverance; he is greedy, avaricious, stubborn, patient, and supercilious." Makhzumi, *Khatirat,* p. 131.

[26] 'Azma, "al-Jami'ah," p. 65. Numerous letters to the editor published in *al-Muqtataf* and *al-Hilal* express the same sentiment; for example, a letter by a lady from Syria ends with these words: "I wish I had died long ago; I would have been spared the sight of the 'Europeanized' women." *al-Hilal,* vol. III (1895), p. 657.

ans are naturally predatory, that "western man feels superior to the nonwestern peoples."[27] He referred to the aggressiveness of Europeans both in Europe and in other parts of the world and attacked Dutch, English, and French imperialism.[28] The West's final goal, he asserted, was to expand its power and to extend its rule over the entire world. Its imperialism was an expression of an innate carnivorous impulse.[29]

Western ill-will. No trust could be placed in the West. "They [the western countries] bargain over our land without our ever having a say in the matter . . ."[30] Whatever western leaders publicly or privately declared, they were not to be believed. Apart from its political and economic ambitions, the West was feared as a dominating culture, as an evil destructive force, undermining everything it touched; for it not only subjugated peoples but it corroded the very foundations of their lives. "Witness what they have done in Africa, [it] saddens the heart and brings tears to one's eyes."[31]

False civilization. Was the West really civilized? The West's spiritual poverty was pointed out again and again.[32] There was a prevalent feeling that western wealth and power were but a veneer concealing moral decay and spiritual emptiness. 'Azma even rejected the western idea of freedom: "The idea of freedom which Western writers bandy about discriminates between European and Easterner, between Mus-

---

[27] Kawakibi, *Taba'i'*, p. 108. Al-Nadim separately developed the same theme: "Non-Western peoples appear as if they have no rights in this world, as if they have no wish to enjoy sovereignty. They stand before Europeans as if they belonged to a different species created only to serve them." *Sulafah*, vol. II, p. 65.

[28] Consciousness of imperialism is related in Kawakibi to nationalism. He viewed the "Arab nation" as extending from North Africa to Iraq. He attacked French imperialism in Algeria "for not allowing Algerians in seventy years of occupation to have one single newspaper of their own." Kawakibi, *Taba'i'*, p. 108.

[29] Afghani (Makhzumi, *Khatirat*, p. 133) employed practically the same argument as the Japanese Aziwa in the *New Proposal*: "When the [western] barbarians plan to subdue a country not their own, they start by opening commerce and watch for a sign of weakness." *Sources of Japanese Traditions*, p. 602.

[30] Statement made in the Ottoman Parliament in 1913 by the Arab representative from Damascus; partial text in Tawfiq 'Ali Birru, *al-'Arab wal-turk fil 'ahd al-dusturi al-'uthmani, 1908–1914* [Arabs and Turks During the Constitutional Period, 1908–1914] (Cairo, 1960), p. 278.

[31] *Ibid.*

[32] The Japanese seemed to have had no doubt about the West's barbarism. Technological advance was to be combined with traditional culture—thus, "eastern ethics and western science," which is a slogan attributed to the modernizing intellectual, Sakuma Shozan (d. 1864). Muslim secularism never achieved this distinction in its denunciation of the West.

lim and Christian, between Protestant and Catholic; according to this idea right seems always to rest with the strong. . . . This is an idea of freedom which should be repudiated and cast away."[33]

There was also the feeling that something was wrong at the heart of western society. Why "do thousands of Europeans become sick of their own civilization?" Because western man had created the very conditions which would lead him to hunger, despair, and death.[34]

When Italy invaded Libya in 1911 (the first European invasion of an Arab country in the twentieth century), a strong wave of anti-European feeling spread throughout Egypt and the Arab provinces of the Ottoman Empire. This seemed to confirm the worst suspicions. The Iraqi poet, Ma'ruf al-Rasafi (d. 1945), wrote a poem which expressed general Arab feeling (it is still frequently quoted today). The East, he said, will henceforth be the victim of the West's mounting aggression. "Do not believe that these are civilized times. They lied to you who told you [that the] leaders of the West. . . . have got anything to tell us but lies, anything to offer us but deceit."[35] Rasafi advised preparation for war, declaring that nothing could protect the Arabs except resistance by force.[36]

The same feeling was echoed by other writers. "Europe feels only hate and enmity toward Islam and the Muslims."[37] "If we expect peace and security at the hands of Europe, then we are lost."[38] And shortly after the war of 1914–18 Rashid Rida wrote to a friend: "I am afraid for the Arabs—not from the Bolsheviks, not from the Turks, but from the British. I am fearful that Britain will now deal the Arabs a crushing blow, before the Arabs have enough time to recover from their prostration."[39]

Power and the Social Problem

There was a tendency among the Muslim secularists to attribute all social evil to some factor causing disfunction in the political system —to tyranny, oppression, imperialism. Hence, the fundamental solu-

[33] 'Azma, al-Durus, p. 47.
[34] In a letter to the editor, the writer concludes with the words: "Thank God, I have never heard of a single instance of an easterner dying of hunger, no matter how poor he might be." al-Hilal, vol. III (1895), p. 698.
[35] 'Ali Mustafa, Muhadarat 'an al-Rasafi [Lectures on al-Rasafi] (Cairo, 1954), p. 52.
[36] "Arise, O East, and prepare for the war to come . . ." Ibid.
[37] Muhammad bin Rahhal al-Jaza'iri, "Mustaqbal al-Islam" [Future of Islam], Majallat al-majallat al-'arabiyyah, vol. II (1902), p. 66.
[38] Shukri Ghanim (d. 1932) in 1913, al-Mu'tamar al-'arabi, p. 145.
[39] Text of letter in Arslan, al-Sayyid Rashid Rida, pp. 314–20.

tions lay not so much in piecemeal programs of reform but in radical adjustment in the power relationship.

This trend placed economic considerations in a secondary position.[40] Political "liberty" was the theme dominating secularist social thought. Quite simply, the Muslim secularists appeared convinced that with the achievement of political liberty a social balance would be automatically achieved. From the viewpoint of this privileged minority, the plight of the impoverished masses was in the natural order of things. The heightened social awareness of Christian intellectualism was, with few exceptions, still lacking in Muslim secularism.

Consciousness of poverty was present; but it found expression not in analysis but in rhetorical declamations. Kawakibi referred to the poor as "the captives of tyranny."[41] Ignorance, together with Ottoman oppression, were the causes of captivity. This led to the conclusion that the overthrow of tyranny was the condition for solving this social ill. The overthrow of tyranny did not necessarily involve violence and bloodshed, however; enlightenment and the eradication of ignorance were equally effective means, for enlightenment and knowledge destroyed fear. And an unfeared tyrant could not be tyrannical; he was thereby transformed into a "guardian" (*wasi*) who learned to love his people and came to cherish their love.[42] Until this happened, however, the poor would remain "powerless and listless captives of tyranny."[43]

The social problem of class inequalities never took definite form in secularist consciousness. From the point of view of the privileged groups, the social structure, with its social and economic stratification, was never questioned. In its attitude toward the masses, Muslim

---

[40] Qasim Amin is an important exception. He held that "the most effective factor in social life is the economic factor." *al-Mar'a*, p. 98.

[41] Kawakibi, *Taba'i'*, p. 29. [42] *Ibid.*

[43] *Ibid.*, p. 99. Generally the plight of the masses was not viewed with sympathy. For example, in a letter to *al-Hilal* dated December 15, 1894, the writer wrote with resentment about the Egyptian peasant's somewhat improved lot. "The fallah is a free man now with no power over him except that of the law. He no longer fears the village chief, not even the governor; he is no longer afraid of the whip. Now that he feels secure he indulges in luxury. In former days he used to live in a thatched hut, now he has built himself a brick house with a wooden roof. . . . In the past he used to sell the milk and cheese and butter he got from his cows; now he sells only what he and his family do not consume. Previously he made his wife do the work which he now uses camels and donkeys to accomplish. . . . In former days he used to eat uncooked greens, now he has meat and chicken to eat. . . . Instead of having only one cotton garment, he now has a woolen mantle and a fez." *al-Hilal*, vol. III (1894), p. 337.

secularism was definitely conservative. It rejected the socialist notions of the radical Christian intellectuals and took refuge in Islamic reformist ideas.

The idea of social justice in Muslim secularist thought rested on the concept of charity. State intervention in social and economic affairs was opposed; rather, the rich had the "religious responsibility" to aid the poor and to bring about cooperation among the various levels of society. Muslim secularist thought posited the principles of *zakat* (charity tax) and *waqf* (religious foundation) as sufficient grounds for bringing about social justice.[44] It defined the means whereby the poor were to be protected from "exploitation by the rich."[45] In the West this was possible only by the coercion of "fanatical socialism."[46] There was not one writer in this group of Muslim intellectuals who favored socialism or who took a positive attitude toward the socialist movement in Europe. Some writers equated socialism with anarchism; their doctrines were portrayed as revolutionary, endangering law and order everywhere.[47] That Europe was threatened from within by socialism was a favorite theme of secularist writers, which afforded much satisfaction. It provided another example of western fallibility and, by contrast, another example of Islam's intrinsic strength.[48]

It is not surprising that the Muslim secularists, like many Christian writers, strongly favored European middle class liberalism. This is evident in their strife to end traditional absolutism, to establish constitutional government and the parliamentary system, and to provide some rational foundation for upholding individual freedom and limiting the power of government. To the secularist elite the concept of constitutionalism meant more than a political order or a system of law. It represented the essential characteristic of civilized society, and provided the condition for this elite's accession to power. The Muslim secularist writers, borrowing from both Christian intellectuals and

---

[44] See Kawakibi, *Tabai'*, p. 56.

[45] Kawakibi (*ibid.*) called for "equalization of rights and uplifting conditions."

[46] "al-Islam wal-madaniyyah" [Islam and Civilization], *al-Muqtabis*, vol. IV (1909), p. 745.

[47] 'Azma, *al-Durus*, p. 42.

[48] Ahmad Lutfi al-Sayyid (d. 1963), the leading Egyptian liberal of his time, urged his countrymen not to surrender to the enticement of socialist ideology. "What we need above all is liberty." *al-Muntakhabat* [Selected Writings] (Cairo, ?-1945), vol. I, p. 63. Revolutionary socialist movements were actively feared by the Muslim secularists. Kurd 'Ali (d. 1953) claimed that socialism was introduced into the Ottoman Empire by Greeks, Bulgarians, and Jews. In 1909 *al-Muqtabis* reported that a socialist party existed in Salonika, and that two socialist newspapers were published in Izmir, one Greek and the other a "Muslim socialist paper." *al-Muqtabis*, vol. IV (1909), p. 744.

Islamic reformists, justified their constitutionalist views by reverting to utilitarian and historicist arguments. Khayr al-Din, quoting extensively from medieval authorities, had demonstrated that "consultative" government (*shura*) was precisely that form of government enjoined by the Qur'an and the Hadith.[49] Kawakibi now developed the argument that the essential structure of government in Islam was "democratic and representative" and that "absolutist rule" was a corruption of these principles and was established after the rise of the Ummayad Empire.[50] In this agrument Muslim secularism was in agreement with the basic premises of Islamic revivalist theory as set forth by Islamic reformism. The utilitarian argument regarded parliamentary government, and the laws and institutions that went with it, as the *sine qua non* not only of political freedom but of the viable modern state, so that the principle of constitutionalism acquired in Muslim secularist thought somewhat the same place that the myth of pristine Islam and that of the modern West had in Islamic reformism and Christian intellectualism, respectively.

Until World War I Muslim secularism took a slightly different course in Egypt from the one it took in the Fertile Crescent. In the Ottoman Empire the failure of constitutional restoration (1908–14) led to the progressive estrangement of the Arab secularist elite from the established order. By 1914 the "liberal" order instituted by the Young Turks was strongly opposed by the young and increasingly nationalistic generation of Muslims. Resistance to the policy of Ottomanization created an opposition to the new regime as strong as that previously directed against Abdul Hamid's oppressive rule. The Turkish "betrayal" of constitutional liberties served in both instances to strengthen the secularists' attachment to the idea of constitutional government. The appeal to the ideas and structures of political liberalism was strongest in the Fertile Crescent at precisely the moment when it emerged out from under Turkish domination in 1918—that is, shortly before it fell under the domination of England and France.

In Egypt opposition to British rule produced essentially the same kind of experience: political frustration only served to enhance the liberal nostalgia. What the Muslim secularists really wanted was not total transformation of the social order, but only its modification. It was the promised constitutional liberties and rights that insured free-

---

[49] *Masalik*, p. 13.

[50] Kawakibi favored a middle position. He regarded constitutional monarchy as the best form of government—"the mean between the two extremes, despotism and republican government." *Umm al-qura* (Cairo, 1894), pp. 21, 27.

dom and the equitable distribution of power and prestige among their stratum.

It appears that this type of liberalism remained a vague ideological trend framed by the interests of the social group that gave it voice. Thus on the level of theory it had no systematic doctrine or program, only slogans; and on the practical level, it fell prey to frustrations caused by their failure to translate wish into reality. But in the end it is probable that constitutional democracy would not have survived anyway in a society lacking a broad-based middle class and deprived of political autonomy.[51]

Despite its ultimate failure, Muslim secularist ideology left its liberal imprint on Arab political consciousness. It made a certain contribution to reasonableness and moderation in political life, and it infused Arab nationalism with a generally antitotalitarian spirit.[52]

[51] On still another level constitutional democracy was difficult to realize because it did not fulfill another condition which Hegel pointed out. "The substantial way of willing, the duty and obligation acknowledged by the subjects themselves," were lacking. *Philosophy of History* (New York, 1954), p. 102.

[52] E.g., "The goal of civilized society is to insure for the individual the maximum of independence and freedom." Amin, *al-Mar'a*, p. 28. "Experience has shown that freedom is the source of good for man; it is at the basis of his social progress and the condition of his moral perfection." *Ibid.*, p. 69. "All our present problems, whether moral or economic or political have their cause in our lack of genuine freedom." al-Sayyid, *al-Muntakhabat*, vol. II, p. 66. "Every right which the government arrogates to itself, it takes away from its subjects. And every increase in its power means increase of its pressure on the freedom of individuals." *Ibid.*, p. 65. And Khayr al-Din, nearly half a century earlier, had observed: "Freedom is the base in which knowledge and civilization . . . are grounded." *Masalik*, p. 95.

Chapter VII. Arab Intellectuals and Political Action

Islamism, Ottomanism, and Nationalism

What was the significance of the ideological orientation of the Arab intellectuals for their concrete political commitments? In order to answer this question it is necessary first to clarify certain basic points.

Before 1914 political involvement and the attitudes to which it gave rise were determined by three main political forces that were dominant in Egypt and the Fertile Crescent: Islamism, Ottomanism, and nationalism. From the substantive standpoint, these political forces and the ideas they represented can be differentiated on more than one level. For the purposes of our discussion the primary level is the relationship between these ideas and the specific groups of Arab intellectuals. Apart from the obvious affinity of certain groups to a given idea, no group may be exclusively identified with any of these three ideas. There was no rigid, one-way relationship between political attitudes and social position (and its corresponding mental outlook); nor, by the same token, was ideological orientation the sole factor determining types of political thinking and conduct. Thus, for example, Islamism to be properly understood in the context of this relationship should not be regarded exclusively in terms of the group of Islamic reformists who gave it its ideological formulation, but also in terms of its political goals. Though the idea of Islamism, like the idea of nationalism and the idea of Ottomanism, may be associated with a specific group outlook, as a political force it was not the monopoly of any one group.

This consideration throws direct light on the causes of the fundamental diversity between Arab intellectualism and its various political orientations. In the absence of basic conditions for conceptual unity, Arab intellectual leadership could anchor itself in no universally acceptable movement or principle, neither on the plane of political thought nor on that of political action. In this respect, Arab intellectual leadership stood in strong contrast to Japanese leadership of the corresponding period of change (Meiji period).[1]

[1] In Japan the response to the western challenge was based on action undertaken by a group of leaders who were able to achieve a workable

If what was good for the Arab nation could not be defined in a way that could win consensus, it was not merely because views differed as to what constituted "good." Disagreement ultimately lay in ambiguity regarding the nature of the national entity itself. Who are we? Muslims? Ottoman? Arabs? Egyptians? Christians?

Let me define the terms more closely. On a level of generality, the idea of Islamism would refer to a specifically religious school of thought based on the conception of Islamic revival; that of Ottomanism to an essentially political idea anchored in an established political reality seeking goals defined strictly in terms of this reality; and that of nationalism to a set of secular values and political goals opposed to both Islamism and Ottomanism.

Opposition was strongest between the Islamic idea and the idea of nationalism. For Islamism basic identification was to be found in the religious *corpus*—the ultimate differentiating factor which gave the definitive answer to the "Who are we?" Nationalism not only relegated this element to a secondary position but transformed it into a cultural factor. Nevertheless, the two conceptions had this important peculiarity in common: they both ultimately based their claim on a "step backward."[2] Both could look to history and cultural heritage for their origin, which caused them to be animated by essentially similar categories of thought and feeling. It is here that the two ideas touched and then separated. Certainly, Islamism contained elements of nationalism. Partly unconsciously, but also partly in self-defense, the new elements were integrated in the old patterns.[3] A specifically Islamic "nationalism" thus made its appearance. At this point the distinction between religion and nationhood was somewhat blurred: in any case, for the broad masses nationalism and Islam were indistinguishable. The secret of Islam's hold on the political realm (which has persisted to the present despite the continual secularization of society) lay

---

definition of the "national good." Despite all differences, there was common allegiance to basic values, among which "emperor" and "nation" were paramount. The goal of modernization was to bring about economic and technological change that would put Japan on a level of equality with the rich and powerful nations of the West. Hand in hand with modernization went military preparedness; hence the slogan: "Enrich the nation and strengthen its arms."

[2] A step backward "points to a present whose origin still awaits remembrance in order to become a beginning which breaks upon the dawn." Martin Heidigger, "Who is Nietzsche's Zarathustra?" *The Review of Metaphysics,* vol. XX (March, 1967), p. 416.

[3] The mode in which this was achieved naturally required the preservation of traditional values and norms. Here the conception of an activist Islamic nationalism comes closest to the Japanese conception, which was based on combining traditional values and western techniques.

precisely in its capacity to see the sacred and the profane interchange-
ably, in terms of the same scale of values.[4]

The development of the spirit of nationalism followed an almost
opposite direction. To the same extent that it freed itself from traditional and religious ties it was more able to express itself in terms of
strictly secular values and goals. A fundamental determinant in the
development of the spirit of nationalism in Egypt was European
imperialism: it was nourished primarily in resistance to Europe. In
the Fertile Crescent the nationalist conception was formed under
different conditions: it was Turkish oppression rather than European
imperialism that accompanied the crystallization of the idea of nationalism. The nationalist movement in Egypt took a unitary and
popular form, with the result that when the Egyptian revolution broke
out in 1919 it could galvanize the entire Egyptian people. In the
Fertile Crescent and Arabia the nationalist movement took not one
but many forms, and none of them succeeded in providing the
grounds for a united movement. The balkanization of the Fertile
Crescent following World War I was carried out by Britain and
France with only sporadic and fragmentary nationalist resistance.

Ottomanism represented an essentially contingent force; its fate
was inextricably bound up with that of the Ottoman polity. When this
was submerged by the war of 1914–18 the Ottoman idea completely
disappeared with it. But of the three dominant political forces of the
prewar period Ottomanism had the strongest foundations and, at least
in the Fertile Crescent, represented the decisive power in political life.

Ottomanism meant different things from different standpoints—according to whether one was an Egyptian, a Muslim Arab, a Christian
Arab, or a non-Arab Muslim. The aspect of Ottomanism that was
most meaningful from all standpoints was its supranational, suprareligious, supraethnic character. It embraced within its political framework all the different nationalities, religions, and ethnic elements in
the empire and provided them with a basis for a workable political
and social system. As the embodiment of a concrete political reality,
Ottomanism had special significance for the upper social strata of all
the various groups (*millet*). It was in the interest of these strata to
protect and maintain the established system. For the educated urban

---

[4] Ideas pertaining to the various schools of thought survived precisely
because they could be accommodated to different attitudes: Hamidian pan-
Islamism, the Islamic activism of Afghani, and Arab Islamic nationalism (of
Muslim secularism and the Hashemite revolt of 1916) constituted closely knit
forces that belonged to the same broad spectrum. Though fully secularized,
even contemporary Arab nationalism, in its Ba'th, Nasserist, and "Socialist"
versions, is shot through and through with religious notions.

Muslims in particular, the Ottoman idea represented the best means to achieve power and status and privilege. At the same time, the Ottoman framework did not negate national or sectarian interests. Indeed, given the realities of political power in the empire, this framework provided the best conditions for the fulfillment of these interests, at least as far as the upper social and religious strata were concerned. From the point of view of many Muslim and Christian Arab intellectuals in the Fertile Crescent some sort of autonomous Arab existence within a decentralized administration was not only possible under Ottomanism, but highly desirable. But Ottomanism, though formally neutral as far as the ethnic-religious factor was concerned, was nevertheless profoundly influenced in its practical orientations by the supremacy of the Islamic and (increasingly after 1910) Turkish elements within the empire.

Nationalism proved, depending on the specific form it took, amenable to a variety of accommodations with the other two dominant forces of political life. For many Muslim and Christian intellectuals there was not necessarily a contradiction between the ideas of nationalism and Ottomanism. Similarly, for many Muslim Arab nationalists the concept of Arabism in a certain sense encompassed the idea of Islam. And many Christian intellectuals were willing to accept a cultural definition of Islam provided it preserved the secular character of nationalism. But polarity remained between the nationalism of the religiously oriented, conservative older generation and that of the secular, western-oriented younger generation. Truly secular nationalism remained outside the mainstream of political activity and was regarded with suspicion by the Ottoman conservative and Muslim reactionary elements alike.

Until several years after World War I the nationalist movement in Egypt took a different course from that which it took in the Fertile Crescent. Egyptian nationalism derived from the lower middle classes, and its ideological formulations were molded by resistance to western political and social and economic domination. The nationalist spirit generally favored both Ottomanism and Islamism on practical and theoretical grounds: they were natural allies in the struggle for independence and against western domination. Egypt's peculiar experience kept it largely isolated from the stream of Arab nationalism in the Fertile Crescent, which flowered under the dual impact of the Arab literary revival and the Christian-mediated ideas of secular nationalism. In Egyptian nationalism the religious stress produced by the actuality of foreign domination contributed to obscuring the Arab perspective, while the literary emphasis produced under the influence

of Christian westernizing thought helped to imprint the Arab character on the nationalism of the Fertile Crescent. It is not accidental that
the revolution of 1952 and the end of British domination in Egypt
have led to the transformation of Egyptian nationalism into Arab
nationalism.

The Political Forms of Islamism

In the West Islamism is often associated with Muslim fanaticism,
pan-Islam, and holy war. These associations have derived from Hamidian pan-Islamic policies, the Mahdist uprising in the Sudan, the
Wahhabi resurgence in Arabia, and similar developments occurring in
the latter part of the nineteenth century and early part of the twentieth. But these conceptions have also been strengthened by inherent
cultural hostility toward the Muslim world.

In reality the idea of Islamism has little to do with western stereotypes about Islam. In its fundamental impulses Islamism was neither
fanatical nor chauvinistic. Its "step backward" outlook was in reality
a nostalgia for an ideal that could be set forth in Muslim terms. Its
ideological formulations represented a political appeal, a call for
action based on a utopian interpretation of Islamic doctrine. In
stressing its own positive values it strove to block the external ones it
thought inimical to revival. Though it dreamed of the restoration of
Islamic power it was not inclined toward violence; rather it put its
trust in the bonds of brotherhood joining all Muslims and saw in
Islamic unity the essential condition for putting a stop to Europe's
aggression.

Politically, Islamism expressed itself in varying forms, all of which
had basic features in common. Certainly the most important form was
the one elaborated by Afghani and his school. Afghani's conception
of Islam extended beyond the confines of the Ottoman Empire and
the Arab world. His idea of the Muslim world was truly universalist
and included all Muslim countries from Southeast Asia to the Atlan-
tic. He was not a dreamer but a shrewd political visionary who was
keenly aware of the political realities of the day. He supported the
official pan-Islamic policy of Abdul Hamid, but, aware of the special
position of the Arabs in the empire and the Muslim world, he
presented his own pro-Arab political scheme. He called for dividing
the empire into semi-autonomous entities (into what he termed "khe-
dival states") and for adopting Arabic, the language of the Qur'an, as
the official language. The caliphate was to remain vested in the house
of Othman. He hoped that Iran, Afghanistan, and Muslim India
would join the Ottoman and Arab countries in a pan-Islamic union.

He was in favor of giving up the Balkan territories altogether and confining Ottoman dominion to Asia and Africa, thus breaking away completely from Europe. He also called for establishing the capital of Islam in Baghdad.[5]

Arab exponents of Islamism were to some extent or another all influenced by Afghani's ideas. But on the whole the Arab spokesmen of political Islamism found it difficult to embrace his universalist view. From the Arab standpoint, the heart of Islam always was the Arab world; the non-Arabic-speaking world of Islam was all, save Turkey, peripheral. Islamic unity signified primarily the unity of Arabs and Turks.

Two of the most vocal Arab Islamists of this period came from Lebanon: Shakib Arslan (d. 1946) and Muhammad Rashid Rida (d. 1935). Though Arslan was not particularly religious, he was wholeheartedly dedicated to the idea of the Islamic state; he wanted to see Islam able to stand up to Europe which he passionately detested.[6] His ideas came close to Afghani's, but like many Arab Islamists he stood for firm ties with Ottomanism. In Arslan, Islamism and Ottomanism found one of their strongest exponents. Rida's conception of Muslim power tended more in the direction of a religious revival than of political unity. Unlike Arslan, he was opposed to Ottomanist rule and could not reconcile himself to Ottoman supremacy, whether religious or political. In *al-Manar* he examined at great length the various grounds on which Islamic unity could be established, and in the end he opted for Wahhabism.

There was another form of Islamism which was particularly strong in the Muslim Sunni circles of Syria and Iraq. It expressed itself in characteristically nationalist terms and came quite close to identifying Arabism (nationalism) with Islamism.[7] It took root shortly before World War I and gained momentum with the outbreak of the Hashimite Arab revolt in 1916. It combined the secular aspirations of the younger Muslim elite and the religious fervor of the traditionalist groups. As a political ideology this form of Islamism reflected the social and psychological conditions that dominated Muslim society in the Fertile Crescent during the turning point of the Arab Awakening. However, despite its nationalist orientation, this form of Islamism

---

[5] Makhzumi, *Khatirat,* pp. 237–41.

[6] He had to spend a good portion of his life exiled in Europe because he was not allowed by the French mandatory to return to his native Lebanon, which he did not see again until shortly before his death.

[7] "Islamism cannot succeed without Arabism, and Arabism cannot succeed without Islamism. To destroy either one is to destroy the other." al-Bani, *Tanwir,* p. 48.

firmly based itself on religious grounds. Many Arab Muslims, even those who considered themselves nationalists, saw no contradiction between Arab nationalism and Islamic unity. This partly accounts for the persistent ambiguity within all forms of Arab nationalism in the Fertile Crescent.

The various forms of Islamism, whether emphasizing the universalist aspect of unity or its Ottoman or Arab character, were all based on a religious view of society. Even the Arab nationalist form of Islamism (as represented, for example, by the Hashimite revolt) adhered to the Muslim concept of nation (*ummah*) which dismissed ethnic and linguistic differentiations and recognized Islam as the distinctive element of national identity.[8] But Islamism, in this as in other forms, revived the medieval view which held mankind to be divided into essentially two groups, Muslims (believers) and non-Muslims (non-believers). It provided the conviction that, by reinstating in political terms the distinction of belonging to Muhammad's people (*ummat Muhammad*), it was possible to restore to Islam its power and position in the world. It implicitly revitalized the spirit of a conquering Islam. Islamism would not only change the attitude of Muslims but also their real relationship to the world. It would transform the entire structure of Islam's confrontation with the West and set it on an altogether different basis.

In terms of politics perhaps the most significant aspect of this emphasis was the opposition between the Islamic notion of a religiously defined *ummah* and the nationalist conception of a secularly defined *nation*. The nationalist view, especially as elaborated by Christian intellectuals, emphasized the social and historical factors. Religion as such was regarded as a supranational principle which should not interfere with loyalty to the nation; individuals belonged to the same nation, not by virtue of common religion but despite religious differences. Thus, inevitably, Islamism constituted from the nationalist point of view an obstacle to national unity. At the time, when Christian intellectuals had already succeeded in breaking down some of the major barriers separating Christian Arab from Muslim Arab, and when some of the Muslim secularists had already become somewhat aware of the essential differences separating Arab from non-Arab Muslims, Islamism was still putting forth its religious claims. Islamism had to reject this secularist nationalism; it saw it as a

[8] According to Rida, for example, "fatherland" and "nation" have strictly religious connotations. "By fatherland we mean all those countries inhabited by the [Muslim] nation." See Mughrabi, introduction to *al-Bayyinat*, vol. II, p. iv. To this day a Saudi or Moroccan Arab finds it difficult to regard as Arab a Lebanese or a Syrian or an Iraqi Christian.

major adversary. Inevitably, nationalism was branded as an alien and heretical product of Europe.[9]

Far from denying it, Islamism stressed the supranational character of Islam.[10] Though men were differentiated in terms of religious faith, they were essentially united by their humanity. Belief in God and adherence to ethical principles superceded all accidental differences and were sufficient grounds for unity. Afghani predicted that one day world peace and world unity will be achieved on the basis of the essential "agreement of the three great religions in their [ethical] principles and goals."[11]

The characteristic feature of all political forms of Islamism was its apocalyptic mentality. In contrast to the rational perspective characteristic of the Christian conception of nationalism, Islamism posited total transformation in apocalyptic terms; change came about not as a result of a coherent sequence but as a sudden upsurge.

This is best exemplified by the vision of a resurrected Islam bursting in on the world. In this vision history was no longer in the past; rather, it became a living contemporary reality that would one day transform the present. It was imbued with an inner force that would suddenly and inexplicably explode into the world of everyday experience.[12] Islamism strengthened the magic-laden mentality: The miraculous became an element of the political attitude; to a certain extent, it still is today.

The various forms of Islamism developed no systematic and unified political vision; there was no elaboration of rational concepts which could lead to the evolution of a coherent doctrine. The pietistic

---

[9] For an eloquent exposition, see Rida's Introduction to the reprinted vol. IX (1906) of al-Manar. "We are told [by the nationalists] that there is no hope for Muslims under the present millet system, that to reconstruct an Islamic state in modern times is impossible, that unless Muslims build their life on national foundations they will have no political life at all, that unless they follow in Europe's footsteps they will have no part in modern civilization. . . ." (p. 8). In 1897 Rida had stated clearly: "Our future depends on rejecting Europe's principle of nationality." al-Manar, vol. I (1897), p. 67.

[10] Louis Massignon was distressed with nationalist incursions into religion and insisted with the Islamists that "l'Islam ne doit pas être 'arabisme,' il est supranational." See Vincent Monteil, Parole donnée (Paris, 1962), p. 15.

[11] Makhzumi, Khatirat, p. 82. Afghani, unlike many Islamists, maintained the distinction between temporal and spiritual power. p. 39.

[12] The coup d'etat may perhaps be viewed as related to this concept; the turn of the tide was to come about as a result of sudden, swift coups that would transform the status quo. For Mughrabi, for example, the new era in the Ottoman Empire began with the coup d'etat of 1908. He saw the same sudden change coming about in Morocco and Afghanistan: "The coup d'etat [inqilab] will take place in these two countries without any doubt, if not right away, soon." al-Bayyinat, vol. II, p. 2.

character of Islamism eliminated the possibility of critical thought and encouraged a rhetorical stance. Traditional values were reinstated by eloquent repetitiveness, and the impulse to change was subdued.

In its reformist-fundamentalist aspect, as in its political-activist aspect, modern Islam could not carry out the task demanded by rapid change. It failed to reformulate fundamental Islamic ideas in modern terms; it could not comprehend change and was thus unable to justify or accommodate it.

Christian Arabs and Political Commitment

As we have seen, Christian intellectualism provided the most fertile ground for the growth of secular nationalism. The political ideas of Christian Arab intellectuals were conditioned by a number of factors, of which perhaps the most important was the political environment of the Christian communities of the Fertile Crescent and Egypt.

Because political differentiation was based on religious grounds, the political organization of Christian communities was closely linked to the denominational structure. The *millet* (religious denomination) system constituted the political and administrative foundations of the Ottoman Empire. As a member of the Christian *millet,* the Christian Arab intellectual was placed somewhat outside the specifically Muslim political order. His duties and rights were prescribed by the communal system and his relationship with the political community at large was determined by his sectarian affiliation.

Of decisive significance to political attitude and behavior was geographic location. Though strictly speaking the *millet* system had no territorial designation, all Christian denominations were to some extent identified by their geographical distribution. Thus, to take an important example, the concentration of Maronite Christians in Mount Lebanon was of crucial significance to the social and psychological genesis of a specifically Maronite attitude. The rugged terrain of Mount Lebanon, which made it virtually invulnerable to invasion, and its proximity to the Mediterranean, which made Europe accessible, were decisive in shaping Maronite political orientation. The Maronites of Lebanon, perhaps more than any other Arab Christian community in the Fertile Crescent, were for centuries able to maintain some form of autonomy amid the surrounding sea of Muslims. In the age of revival this provided the grounds for the elaboration of a distinct conception of nationality based on what might be called sectarian territoriality—which eventually led to the emergence of the idea of a Lebanese nationality.

In contrast, the political orientation of the Greek Orthodox Christians, the largest Christian Arab *millet* in the Fertile Crescent, took on a somewhat different character. This was in great part due to the demographic diffusion of Greek Orthodox Christians throughout Syria and their lack of concentration in any one area. They mixed more easily with their Muslim surroundings and were consequently able to accommodate themselves to Arabism in a way that most other Christian groups could not. An independent, specifically Greek Orthodox conception of nationality was hard to evolve under these circumstances. What did develop in fact was a distinctive Greek Orthodox conception of Arab nationality which made it possible for Greek Orthodox Christians to identify more readily with their Muslim Arab compatriots than any other Christian group was ever able to do. It is therefore not surprising that the Greek Orthodox Christians assumed political attitudes that were generally much closer to Arabism than they were to political sectarianism.

In those areas where Christian Arabs constituted a majority, or where they constituted sizable, contiguous minorities, as they did in the coastal cities and towns from Antioch to Jaffa, they normally enjoyed ample opportunities to engage in politics. In areas where they constituted small minorities amid a Muslim majority they tended to withdraw from participation in public and political life. This generally held true for the Christian communities of the interior. The Christian minorities in Iraq, for example, owing to their structural diversity, small size, and social isolation, tended to lead a closed-in and parochial existence with little contact with their Muslim environment. In this category, with certain exceptions, may be included the large Coptic Christian community in Egypt. The Egyptian Copts, like the Christians of Iraq, constituted a socially fossilized group. They were inhibited by their environment from playing a significant role in political life.

Life in Egypt provided a unique type of social environment for a significant number of Christian intellectuals. During the period after World War I the Syrian Christian community in Egypt grew rapidly in number and importance. Belonging to the foreign community and having most of the privileges and immunities of the Europeans in Egypt, the Christian writers and publishers enjoyed probably the greatest freedom of thought and expression experienced anywhere by any group of Arab intellectuals in the twentieth century. Ideological commitment came naturally to all those with a mature political consciousness, and the ideological positions taken by them ranged from total abstention from political involvement to passionate and total engagement.

The political attitude of Christian Arabs both in Egypt and the Fertile Crescent was strongly determined by their social status. It may be said that generally the more privileged strata were the ones more likely and able to participate in political life. In this case, political attitudes tended to be mostly governed by particular interests. Thus the great feudal families of Lebanon, the big merchants of Beirut or Aleppo, and the educated middle class elite of the coastal towns were all strongly influenced in their political attitudes by the "material" and "ideal" interests of their specific situation. As situations changed so did attitudes and orientations. Belonging to the intelligentsia bestowed its own privileged position as well as its own interests. The attitudes of intellectuals were indicative of the social or political interests with which they identified themselves. Naturally, for intellectuals the determining factors were predominantly ideological. Indeed the significance of the role of the intellectuals consisted precisely in this propensity to identify political participation and commitment with various concrete interests and motivations and to articulate them in ideological forms.

The Arab literary revival provided the logical base for the political revival. To them, language, and the cultural heritage in which it was embedded, constituted the basis of national identity: "We are all brothers in our homeland, joined together by the common bond of language," wrote Adib Ishaq.[13] Arabs, both Muslim and Christian, constituted a single cultural entity. "Awake ye Arabs and arise," proclaimed the Christian Arab poet, Ibrahim al-Yaziji.

Neither Yaziji, nor Ishaq, nor any other of the early Christian literati consciously thought of themselves as Arab nationalists. But the concept of Arabism, though it signified at this early stage purely cultural and literary values, implied a decisive differentiation which expressed itself in new criteria of self-identification. It eventually based itself on new grounds of loyalty; to the concept of identity was added the correlative idea of territoriality: "Love of country is a kind of faith" (Butrus Bustani); "God belongs to religion but the fatherland belongs to everyone." Religion and nation were no longer part of a single, inseparable reality. The former was now regarded as belonging to a private personal realm, the latter to the public collective realm. They felt that the distinction between Muslim and Christian should no longer be relevant politically, for there was only one people, one country, one destiny.[14] It soon became clear that national

[13] See 'Abboud, *Ruwwad,* p. 188.
[14] Christian intellectuals attributed the distinction between *Christian* and *Muslim* Arabs to prejudice and European imperialism. Sulayman Bustani

integration depended upon the elimination of religious differentiation and its replacement by the national principle.[15]

In terms of active political involvement, there were four positions which characterized Christian political attitude. The first was based on complete espousal of the idea of Ottomanism. The adherents to this principle usually belonged to the social stratum that stood to gain most from the preservation of the status quo—the big landlords, the higher clergy, the great urban families, and those individuals and groups who had a stake in the established order. The unity of all sects and ethnic and national groups of the Ottoman Empire and the Ottoman status quo was upheld. Adherents advocated submission to the established order and opposed all kinds of resistance. Religion and nationality were subordinated to the *millet* system and absorbed into the Ottoman supercommunity: one could be Arab and Christian, but his essential identity was defined in terms of Ottomanism.[16]

Sulayman Bustani provided what was probably the most important rationalization of the Ottomanist position. He openly upheld the principle of Muslim Ottoman ascendancy; the non-Muslim subjects of the empire were advised to acknowledge this fact and accommodate

---

declared that "it is the foreigners who by education divide our minds and by power divide our lands." *'Ibrah,* p. 38. The same view was later set forth by other Christian intellectuals; e.g., As'ad Daghir (d. 1935): "The truth is acknowledged by every responsible man, namely, that this prejudice was introduced into the Arab world and into Islam by the foreigners to achieve their goals. . . . Thus the foreign schools which were established in the Arab countries since the beginning of the nineteenth century are centers for propagating religious bigotry and communal hatred aiming at breaking up the Arab nation into warring factions and sects each trying to destroy the other . . ." *Mudhakkirati 'ala hamish al-qadiyyah al-'arabiyyah* [Memoirs on the Arab Question] (Cairo, n.d.), p. 28.

[15] Islamism was bitterly opposed to this principle. Muslim secularism, on the other hand, welcomed it wholeheartedly; e.g., Mustafa Kamil: "Muslims and Copts constitute one people; they are bound together by the ties of patriotism, by custom and tradition, and by the same way of life. They can never be separated from one another." 'Abdul-Rahman al-Rafi'i, *Mustafa Kamil ba'ith al-harakah al-wataniyyah* [Mustafa Kamil, the Founder of the National Movement] (3rd. ed.; Cairo, 1950), p. 101. See also Kawakibi: "Let us attend to our life on this earth and leave religion to take care of the hereafter. Let this be our motto: 'Long live the nation, long live the fatherland.' " *Taba'i',* p. 107.

[16] "Egyptians, Hijazis, Iraqis, Syrians, Armenians, Anatolians, Tripolitanians, Cretans, and Bulgarians are all brothers, children of one mother, the Ottoman state, of one father, his Majesty the Sultan. Indeed, every Arab, Turk, Armenian, and Circasian belongs to one nationality: he is an Ottoman ['uthmani]; every Muslim, Jew, Christian, Druze belongs to one nationality: he is an Ottoman." He who distinguished himself or his people in religious or national terms "was a traitor to his religion . . . and his country." Salim Taqla (d. 1892), *"al-Jami'a al-'uthmaniyyah"* [Ottoman Unity], *Majali,* ed. Sufayr, p. 74.

themselves to it. Their religious and communal interests as well as their social well-being depended on the degree and sincerity of their loyalty to the empire. Bustani stood for complete Ottomanization and advocated combating all forms of particularisms, whether sectarian or national. He seemed genuinely convinced that the Ottoman social structure and its political organization were sound and effective. He called for lifting the ban on conscription of Christians (so that they could fight shoulder to shoulder with their Muslim compatriots) and for making Turkish the official language in the Arab provinces.[17]

Another Christian position called for a modification (reform) of the status quo without undermining it; it found its strongest expression in the movement for administrative decentralization. The idea of Turkish hegemony was rejected. It was stressed that the national differences among the various peoples of the empire entitled them to a measure of internal independence and administrative autonomy.[18] In this movement we see the beginnings of organized political opposition carried out from within the Ottoman structure in the name of national identity. For this movement to achieve any success it was essential to receive the backing not only of important Christian groups but also of Muslim Arabs. The decentralists strongly rejected precisely those elements of the *millet* system which pro-Ottoman Christians such as S. Bustani had emphatically stressed; they attacked the status quo by outlining what the natural consequences of Ottoman unity would be: if the various *millets* of the empire were to give up their own identity in favor of the common Ottoman identity, then no group (i.e., the Turks) would have a privileged position in the established order. "We want an *Ottoman* government, not a Turkish or an Arab government, a government in which all communities of the Ottoman empire have equal rights and equal duties."[19] Actually, the Christian decentralists wanted more than mere reform of the *millet* system. By underscoring political equality they invoked a new principle—the right to administrative autonomy within the *millet* structure. But the only way this argument could be pressed on was by relegating the religious element to the background and by insisting on

[17] He went so far as to suggest that Arabic be replaced by Turkish as the principal language of instruction in the schools.

[18] This view was comprehensively articulated at a general conference held in Paris in 1913 sponsored by the Party of Ottoman Decentralization. "We Ottoman subjects have more need for decentralized administration than any other people in the world, because [the Ottoman Empire] is composed of different [national and religious] minorities that differ from one another in ethnic origin, language, historical background." *al-Mu'tamar,* p. 100.

[19] *Ibid.,* p. 104.

the national element. By clinging to a position based on the recognition of Arab identity within the empire the Christian Arab intellectuals strengthened the movement of administrative decentralization and provided the concrete basis for political collaboration between Muslim and Christian Arabs on a nationalist basis.

It must be added that the demand for decentralization did not imply the desire to break away from the Ottoman Empire. Both Christians and Muslims sincerely thought, at least at this stage, solely in terms of internal autonomy; they were convinced that Arab interests were best served by preserving the Ottoman Empire.[20] On this level the Christian decentralist position was opposed to Ottomanism only in terms of modality; it strongly upheld the unity and territorial integrity of the empire.

Christian decentralists were mostly urban dwellers and professionals; the position was also popular with Christian intellectuals living in Egypt and Europe.

A third Christian position expressed itself in a distinctly Arab nationalist attitude which was vigorously opposed to Ottoman domination. This constituted, in effect, the highest stage of political awareness. Its first formulations were made primarily by emigrant Christian intellectuals living in Egypt, Europe, and America.

Probably the first to give a straightforward, unambiguous political (as distinct from cultural or linguistic) definition of the idea of nationality were the Christian expatriates Najib Azoury (d. 1916) and Amin Rihani (d. 1940). Azoury proclaimed as early as 1905[21] that the Arab nation constituted a single independent entity in which Christians and Muslims were equal partners. He was the first to demand a total break with the Ottoman Empire.[22]

But who precisely were the Arabs? What was the exact territorial definition of the Arab *patrie?* When Ishaq and Yaziji spoke of the Arabs they referred in a general way to all Arabic-speaking people; they had no definite territorial designation in mind and thought in

---

[20] For example, Nadrah Mutran, a leading Lebanese Christian at the Paris conference, delivered a speech entitled, "Preserving the National Existence of the Arab Countries in the Ottoman Empire," in which he outlined the Arabs' interest in maintaining their place within the Ottoman Empire. "Our links with the Ottoman state and our relation with the Turkish people are the best safeguards of our interests . . ." *Ibid.,* p. 59.

[21] *Réveil de la nation arabe* (Paris, 1905).

[22] Kawakibi expressed similar ideas, but his anti-Ottomanism derived from his opposition to Hamidian tyranny and his position was based on Islamic revival. Though classified as secularist, Kawakibi was somewhat vague about the problem of separating church and state, as he was about his political conception of Arabism.

cultural rather than in political terms. When the literary sentiment had transformed itself into political awareness, the nationalist conception presented itself in, so to speak, a double focus: the ideas of nation and fatherland did not quite coincide; there was profound ambivalence as to the manner in which one was related to the other. First there was the idea of the Syrian homeland, of which Butrus Bustani wrote so passionately.[23] The sense of Syrian nationhood was the product of early spontaneous political awareness; it attached itself to the definite territorial extension of the Syrian homeland. The Arab conception deriving from the literary renaissance slowly superimposed itself on this Syrian conception, but did not completely efface it. The wider Arab conception required a redefinition of the territorial aspect. Amin Rihani, in a lecture given in 1909 at the Syrian Protestant College in Beirut, supplied this definition: "If you look at the map you will see certain regions occupying a central location in the world. These are Natural Syria, Mesopotamia, and the Arabian Peninsula. These territories constitute our Arab fatherland [*watan*]."[24] Thus the nationalist conception encompassed, from one standpoint, Geographic Syria and, from another, the Arabian peninsula and the Fertile Crescent.[25] Later the Arab conception specifically embraced the entire Arabic-speaking world, including North Africa; and the Syrian conception, at least in its final political embodiment in the Syrian National Movement,[26] included all of the Fertile Crescent. The opposition in Christian political consciousness between the familiar and immediately perceived reality of Syria and the vision of the larger, all-embracing Arab entity gave expression to a profound tension which was later experienced in varying degrees of intensity by all the people of the Arab world. National awareness inevitably brought in its train the polarization between a narrow, "local" nationalism and a larger, all-encompassing, nationalism. This dichotomy is reflected today—both politically and psychologically—in the insurmountable contradictions in every Arab nation-state between the reality of national sovereignty and the idea of greater Arab unity.

[23] In his short-lived newspaper, *Nafir Suriyya* (1860–61), he advocated the national unity of "all Syrians"; the motto of his paper was, "God belongs to religion and the fatherland belongs to everyone." Fatherland here referred to Greater or Geographic Syria.

[24] Text in *al-Muqtataf*, vol. XXXIV (1909), pp. 574–75.

[25] Egypt and Arab North Africa (*al-maghrib*) were not included. Shortly after World War I Rihani traveled throughout the Arabian Peninsula and Iraq and wrote *Muluk al-'Arab* [The Kings of the Arabs] (Beirut, 1922), a best seller in the Arab world.

[26] On this movement, see Labib Z. Yamaq, *The Syrian National Party* (Cambridge, Mass., 1967).

The fourth Christian position was based on a sectarian conception of nationality and was primarily the product of Christian experience in Lebanon. This conception was rooted in a strong sense of estrangement[27] from both Islamism and Arabism, and it found its political expression in the idea of an independent Christian polity. In a certain sense, there was really no other solution for the Christian predicament, except emigration (or conversion to Islam). In Lebanon the tendency toward affirmation of separate Christian identity was the outcome of long historical experience.

The only condition under which Christian nationalism could allow itself to be absorbed by Arab nationalism was the total secularization of the latter; but complete disassociation between Arabism and Islam was, as many Christian Arabs knew, impossible. The interests of various social and religious groups were, of course, instrumental in encouraging sectarian separateness and in pressing for an independent Lebanese entity. Until 1914 Ottomanism offered the best framework for such an entity, for it provided the most favorable conditions for a practical modus vivendi.

Interestingly enough, this orientation gave rise in the home of Christian westernizing intellectualism to a mental attitude that had all the psychological characteristics of Islamism: it was rooted in a religious conception, and it expressed itself politically through the clerical hierarchy. The theocratic concepts which Christian intellectuals had combated were now embodied in the political reality which was Lebanon. In this reality, internal autonomy under Ottomanism served to consecrate feudal privilege and to strengthen the political hold of religious leadership. Just as Islamism oriented itself toward the Muslim nations of the East, Lebanese Christian sectarianism turned toward Europe for protection and aid. By 1914 Christian sectarianism had become politicized; and when, in 1918, the last Turkish troops had withdrawn and the first French contingents landed in Beirut, it openly declared itself opposed to Arab nationalism and with open arms welcomed the French mandate over Syria and Lebanon.

It must be emphasized that Christian sectarians regarded Arabism and Islamism—which were considered more or less synonymous—as hostile to Christianity not only religiously but also culturally.[28] Chris-

[27] As Zaydan put it, Christians "though part of Ottoman society are neither recruited into the army, nor allowed to fight for the Ottoman state. They do not speak Turkish and have nothing to bind them to the Ottoman empire. Syria, their homeland, has no use for them." *Mukhtarat,* vol. III, p. 94.

[28] Edward Atiyeh (d. 1964), a Lebanese Christian who emigrated first to Egypt and later to Britain, gives probably the best expression of this attitude in

tian sectarianism turned its face toward the Mediterranean and Europe and its back to the desert and Islam.[29] Christian sectarians not only considered themselves basically different from their Muslim Arab compatriots and culturally superior to them but they were convinced that to be free it was not enough to be rid of Muslim Turkish rule: it was necessary to have the direct protection of Christian Europe.[30]

The Christian sectarian outlook produced its own myth, but its final elaboration into a distinctively Lebanese national doctrine had to await the French mandate and the establishment of the state of Greater Lebanon in 1920. As a political doctrine, Christian sectarianism had defended itself before 1914 in terms of historical rights and sectarian principles; after the war it established itself on the political reality of Greater Lebanon and opposed Islamism and Syrian and Arab nationalism from a position of equality.

The Political Attitude of Muslim Secularists

For the Muslim secularists of the Fertile Crescent the dominant force to reckon with in political life was Ottomanism. As we have already pointed out, for the Islamic reformists and Christian westernizers the main interest was not so much in concrete power as in an instrumental adjustment to it: The reformists advocated an Islamic unitary ideology, which Ottomanism was in some way committed to uphold; and the Christian westernizers (including sectarians) called for various forms of pragmatic accommodation to Ottoman reality or

---

his autobiography, *An Arab Tells his Story:* "Arab nationalism seemed to us mainly a Moslem affair and we mistrusted it. A few Christians did indeed take part in it, but they were a mere handful and were regarded by the rest as misguided cranks." The transformation of his attitude from Christian sectarian to Arab nationalist reflects a process characteristic of many Christian intellectuals of the first half of the twentieth century.

[29] "The Syrian Christians, particularly the Lebanese, living along the Mediterranean coast in contact with European influences from the earliest times, were a sophisticated people and looked down upon the Arabs of the interior as a primitive race far below them in culture. On cultural grounds, therefore, as well as religious, the Christian Arabs of Syria had no desire to share in an Arab state which they were sure would be backward and reactionary." *Ibid.*

[30] During World War I many Christians hoped for an allied victory. "For us, Syrian Christians," Atiyeh wrote, "the victory of England and her allies would realize a dream we had dreamt for many years, the dream of Syria free from the Turkish yoke and from fear of the Moslems and placed directly under the protection of a European power." *Ibid.* As for the Arab (Hashimite) revolt of 1916: "I knew that the Arabs were in revolt against Turkey, fighting on the side of England and planning to set up an independent Arab state after the war, but we Christians had no real interest in this movement." *Ibid.*

of opposing it. The relation of Muslim secularists to Ottomanism was governed by other more immediate considerations.

From a social point of view the Muslim secularist elite considered itself entitled to an equal share of the power and privilege in the empire. Membership in this group was distinctly defined not in terms of adherence to a specific ideology but rather in terms of affiliation with the privileged strata of Arab society. The interest situation of the Muslim secularist elite received its clearest crystallization after the fall of the Hamidian regime (1908). For this group return to constitutional life signified not only the reinstatement of political liberty, but the restoration of social and political privilege. The struggle for power and the pursuit of individual and group interests tended to create common ideological formulations, but, in practice, political attitudes quite often differed from one individual or group to another.

It was from members of this Muslim secularist generation that, willy-nilly, Arab nationalism received its political leadership. The achievements and final character of the Arab nationalist movement were greatly influenced by the fact that long before it was transformed into a full-fledged political movement it fell under the control of this emerging Muslim elite. For an entire generation the secularist leaders saw their own interests and those of the movement as identical. Their political actions and decisions were not determined by fixed values or long-term objectives, but primarily by group interests and the empirical situation.

As long as this group remained immune from concerted pressure from below, it was able to maintain a monopoly of power and to act in terms of its material and ideological interests. In its approach to political life it bestowed universal value upon what actually constituted a private good.

Inasmuch as the Muslim secularists constituted the focal point in political life during this period, their attitude as a group toward Ottomanism was of great practical significance for all subsequent political developments. Generally speaking, the Muslim secularists exhibited three different attitudes toward Ottomanism: (1) total adherence to the Ottoman idea; (2) total rejection of it; and (3) a conditional accommodation to it, which was the most prevalent attitude.

The tendency toward identification with Ottomanism was characteristic of the religiously oriented and non-Arab elements of the Muslim secularists. For the Arabic-speaking Kurds and Circassians Ottomanism represented a sort of substitute nationality;[31] it provided

---

[31] Two prominent members of this group were Muhammad Kurd 'Ali (d. 1953) and Waliyy al-Din Yakan (d. 1921), both of Kurdish background. Kurd

a political doctrine and a basis for self-identity. In this sense it suggested something more than the empirical reality of the empire: an ideological mystique.

Ottomanism received some of its strongest support by far from those adhering to the Islamic position. In the name of religion this position appealed strongly to Arabs and non-Arabs alike, reinforcing Islam's supranational unity. In this, Ottomanism exerted an effective counterweight to secular nationalism in all of its various forms.[32]

Opposition to Ottomanism was largely confined to those among the Muslim secularists who saw no possibility of reconciling the principle of Ottoman loyalty to that of Arab nationalism. Ottomanism was regarded as an instrument of Turkish domination. Its protestations on behalf of Islam and its claims to supranational loyalty were regarded with deep mistrust.[33] This attitude gained ground shortly after the outbreak of World War I and again following the Turkish repressions in 1915 and 1916.

But the most important part was played by those Muslim secularists who neither wholly rejected Ottomanism nor fully embraced it. Their objective was to achieve a kind of accommodation with it that would assure participation in power and preservation of privilege.

'Ali repudiated Arab nationalism. Yakan, who lived almost all his life in Egypt, wrote: "Some Egyptian writers have said, 'Egypt for the Egyptians'; I say, 'Egypt for the Ottomans.' " *al-Ma'lum wal majhul* (Cairo, 1909–11) I, p. 30. "To my fatherland I am willing to sacrifice everything so long as I live an Ottoman subject and die an Ottoman subject." *Ibid.*, p. 139. But there were Arab intellectuals who stood for Ottomanism. The Iraqi poet Rusafi (d. 1945) was elected to Parliament in 1912 and spent the war in Constantinople. In 1914 he wrote patriotic poems urging the Arabs to fight on the side of the caliphate and against its enemies. See 'Ali, Muhadarat, *'an Ma'ruf al-Rusafi* [Lectures on Ma'ruf al-Rusafi] (Cairo, 1954), p. 53. His contemporary, an equally famous poet, Zahawi (d. 1936), took an opposite position and called upon the Arabs to abandon the Turks and ally themselves with the British (whom he described as "men of justice and truth both in word and deed"). See 'Abdul-Raziq al-Hilali, *al-Zahawi bayn al-thawra wa'l-sukut* [al-Zahawi Between Rebellion and Silence] (Beirut, n.d.), p. 39.

[32] This is mainly the reason why Ottomanism rather than Arabism became the rallying symbol for a Muslim secularist like Shakib Arslan. He saw Islamic unity as the only foundation upon which political action could be built and the Ottoman caliphate as the only power capable of providing this foundation. During the war he collaborated with Kurd 'Ali and Mughrabi in putting out *al-Sharq*, the government newspaper published in Damascus. After the war he upheld a pan-Arab ideology founded upon the principle of pan-Islamism and practically indistinguishable from it.

[33] E.g., by Kawakibi and Jaza'iri. The first opposed it in the name of freedom and the right of people to determine their own destiny. The latter opposed it from an Islamic position which based itself on an Arab conception. Jaza'iri, like so many other exiles, returned to Damascus in 1908 but went back again to Egypt convinced that Ottoman hegemony represented nothing else but Turkish domination of the Arabs. His attitude, however, was rather uncommon among Islamists.

This took many forms—all eventually ending with failure at accommodation.

The first form was strictly political and started in the Ottoman Parliament. In 1911 Arab and other national elements in the Parliament protested against the Turkish monopoly of power and influence. This was followed by large-scale resignations from the ruling C.U.P. party and the formation of an opposition party.[34] The new party called for the establishment of "true Ottomanism," i.e., for the equitable distribution of rights and obligations among the various peoples of the empire. In what was the first formal call for administrative decentralization, it declared that the interests of the provinces were best served by the introduction of local autonomy. It also held that harmony among the different ethnic and religious groups of the empire could best be achieved through proportional distribution of "offices and positions" on both the local and central levels. The party declared itself opposed to the principles of nationalism (al-qawmiy-yah) and Islamism (al-islamiyyah) and for Ottoman unity.[35]

Another form of opposition and accommodation reflected itself in the first Arab Congress, which met in Paris in 1913 to lay down the formal demands for the "administrative decentralization of the empire." The Congress was partly the result of the failure of parliamentary opposition, and was called by the newly founded Party of Ottoman Decentralization, which was established in Cairo.[36] This party was determined to press its attack against the Turkish monopoly of power, but it also made clear its readiness to compromise on the basis of minimum demands. It assumed an uncompromising position concerning internal autonomy: "We wish to inform the Ottoman government that the principle of decentralization is the basis of [Arab] political life . . . that the Arabs are to be regarded as partners in the empire—partners in the army, in the administration, and also in policy making. In their internal affairs they can have no partners, they are the sole holders of that right."[37]

The twelve-point memorandum was submitted to Constantinople

[34] The Party of Freedom and Cooperation (Hizb al-hurriyyah w'al i'tilaf). See Birru, al-'Arab, pp. 301–8. The party had Albanian, Armenian, Greek, and Bulgarian members; it opened branches in major cities and towns of the Fertile Crescent.

[35] Ibid., p. 304.

[36] The text of the party program can be found in al-Manar, vol. XVI (1913), pp. 226–31.

[37] Text in al-Mu'tamar al-'arabi, pp. 7–10. The Congress had four main topics on its agenda: "National Life and Resistence to Occupation," "Arab Rights in the Ottoman Empire," "Reform on the Basis of Decentralization," and "Emigration from and Immigration to Syria." The final resolutions of the Congress were put in a twelve point memorandum.

as embodying the official Arab demands. Special emphasis was placed on the teaching and official status of the Arabic language.[38] Government functions, especially those relating to the "pious foundations" (*waqf*) and local public works, were to be entrusted to local authorities; service in the army was to be confined "as much as possible" to areas from which the soldiers were recruited; municipal councils were to be given an effective voice in all administrative decisions; deficits incurred by the local administration were to be made up from revenue raised locally and accruing to the central government; and foreign advisors were to be appointed "wherever needed" in the local administrative system.

The main burden of the resolutions was concerned with the distribution of positions and offices. It was demanded that "at least three Arabs should be appointed to the Ottoman cabinet"; a number of qualified Arabs should be placed in "the various ministries as counselors and assistants"; two or three Arabs should be appointed members of "the various advisory councils of the state, the high court, and the department of religious affairs [headed by the *Shaykh al-Islam*]"; and, finally, "at least four or five Arabs be appointed to each of the other departments of the central government." It was also demanded that "at least five *walis* and *mutassarifs* [provincial governors] should be appointed from among qualified Arabs, and that at least two Arab notables from each province should be appointed to the upper house of parliament."

The Ottoman government rejected all resolutions connected with office distribution—which amounted to a rejection of the central demands. This rebuff marked the beginning of the collapse of Ottomanism within the leading secular circles.

In the first phase of opposition to Ottoman predominance the idea of Arabism remained in the background; but now it gradually came to the forefront and stood in inevitable opposition to the idea of Ottomanism.

Before World War I, Arab nationalism was regarded by Arab Ottomanists as a conspiracy "aimed at destroying the Ottoman state and bringing down the caliphate."[39] By the outbreak of the war the pendulum had already begun to swing toward the other extreme. The

---

[38] It was demanded that Arabic should be the principal language in all Arab elementary and preparatory schools; that all Ottoman officials below the rank of governor appointed to the Arab provinces be able to speak Arabic; and that Arabic should be the official language in all the Arab provinces of the empire. The text of cable sent to the Ottoman Ministry of the Interior (July 20, 1913) is in *Mu'tamar,* pp. iv–vi.

[39] The "conspiracy" was obliquely attributed to Christians who advocated the nationalist principle, and who opposed Islamism and Ottomanism,

nationalist thrust was now effected by the younger Muslim secularists who had been behind the more radical formulations of the Paris Congress. Unlike their elders, who were inclined to be cautious and conciliatory, they were eager to uphold a fully nationalist position. One of the most articulate spokesmen of this younger secularist group was 'Abdul-Ghani al-'Uraysi, a brilliant Muslim Lebanese law student in Paris.[40] He summed up the nationalist position in these words:

> The question before us is that of national Arab right. The first claim of any collectivity is its right to nationality.
> We are Arabs irrespective of the form of our present political structure. Through the centuries we have preserved our national character and maintained our national identity despite the attempts of the government of Constantinople to absorb us politically, and to exploit us imperialistically, and to dissolve us as a distinct national entity.
> We have taken it upon ourselves to maintain our special position in the Ottoman empire, to safeguard our nationality and to gain complete equality [with the Turks]. The Arab fatherland and the Arab nation will not submit to being exploited. We are no longer a flock of sheep [ra'iyyah] to be fleeced with impunity. We are self-conscious, self-governing citizens.[41]

Once this position was put forth it became increasingly difficult to preserve a position of compromise. Nationalist self-assertion demanded that true identity come before religious or political affiliation. This position was openly advocated on the eve of World War I in equally uncompromising terms:

> We are Arabs before everything else. Muslims are Arab, and Christians are Arab . . . . But we are Arabs before we are Muslims or Christians. . . . We have left religion and prayer in the mosques and the churches. If we are Arabs before being either Muslims or Christians, then is it surprising that we are Arabs before we are Ottomans?[42]

This Arabist trend expressed itself in three organizational forms: the "literary club," the "literary and social society," and the "underground society" or cell.

The literary club was the first conscious step by the Muslim secularists toward a nationalist organization. The mode of expression peculiar to this form was basically nonpolitical. But literary expression served as the first vehicle of conscious political feeling. Signifi-

---

[40] He was hanged in 1915 in the public square of Beirut (henceforth renamed "Martyrs Square"), along with many of his Muslim and Christian compatriots, by order of Jamal Pasha, the Turkish military governor of Syria (1914–18).

[41] Mu'tamar al-'Arabi, p. 42.

[42] From a speech delivered at al-Muntada al-'arabi [The Arab Literary Club] in Constantinople in April, 1913. See al-Ahram, April 22, 1913.

cantly, the first and most important literary clubs were formed in Constantinople.

The societies, which were also predominantly literary in character, represented a more advanced stage of political consciousness. They avoided direct political involvement, but they nevertheless provided the best cover for political activity, whether on the local or national levels.

The underground or secret society was the form devoted exclusively to political action. The first and most important secret society of the prewar period was the Young Arab society (al-jam'iyyah al-'arabiyyah al-fatah), founded in Paris in 1911.[43] This form of organization constituted the basis of Arab opposition to Ottomanism and the springboard for concrete nationalist action.

The part played by the Muslim secularists through these typical forms of organization was decisive for the Arab national awakening. In the Fertile Crescent their confrontation with Ottomanism acted as a major force in molding the political and nationalist trends.[44] Though Ottomanism was finally rejected as a principle of political loyalty, it left an indelible stamp on the style and mentality of this generation. The war obliterated the political framework of Ottomanism but not its psychological traces.

Reared in the Ottoman environment, the Muslim secularists were accustomed to ambivalence. Reality presented itself in appearances; words, not meaning, held sway; in public life the highest goal was attainment of official position. Authority carried with it not responsibility but the opportunity to enhance one's status and wealth. Ritual and ceremony, servility and the indirect approach, were the tools to achieve status and prestige.

For those who refused to subordinate themselves to the Ottoman

[43] This was patterned after Young Italy and other European "secret societies." "We used to worship Cavour and Garibaldi . . ." Sami al-Sulh, *Mudhakkirati* [My Memoirs] (Beirut, 1960), p. 21. *al-Fatah* maintained a quasisecret character until the arrest of its most prominent members in Damascus and Beirut in the spring and summer of 1915. Another important secret society was *al-'Ahd* [Covenant] which was founded in Constantinople in 1913 by Arab army officers serving in the Ottoman army.

[44] The mentality and style of Muslim secularism in the Fertile Crescent differed in certain important respects from those characteristic of Egyptian Muslim secularism. Nominally under Ottoman sovereignty, Egypt remained Ottoman oriented in its political sympathies. Its Muslim secularist leadership was strongly influenced by two factors lacking in the Fertile Crescent: the religious and ethnic homogeneity of Egyptian society, and the geographic unity of the country. This was in great part responsible for the distinctly Islamic tendency of Egyptian nationalism and for the cohesiveness of the Egyptian national movement.

system the problem remained essentially the same: collaboration or exile required the cultivation of the same faculties for survival—dissimulation, intrigue, and compromise. In this generation collaboration did not create traitors, nor exile revolutionaries.

Why did this Muslim secular leadership ultimately fail? In the first place, it never could provide an autonomous ideological foundation of its own: it lacked both the unitary absoluteness of Islamism and the pragmatic rationalism of the Christian westernizers. Its nationalistic stand, whether Egyptian or Arab, never received full elaboration in rational terms. In Egypt the religious element remained paramount, and in the Fertile Crescent the movement succumbed to factional divisiveness. Muslim bourgeois secularism could not achieve real autonomy; in its attitude and activities it was always bound to centers of power and interest outside of itself. Europe, the source of its inspiration and object of its fear, was its master and model. Forced by irreconcilable contradictions to continual retreat, Muslim secularism was foredoomed to collapse by the end of the interwar period, when political domination shifted to the rising petit bourgeoisie—which at that time had become embodied in the bureaucratic and military structures.

Chapter VIII. Arab Intellectuals and the West

Traditional Values and Modern Science

When Japan defeated Russia in 1905 its triumph was joyously hailed throughout the Arab world. It was the first defeat of a western power at the hands of an eastern nation. It was not merely a Japanese victory, but in a psychological sense an Arab, Muslim victory as well.

What made it possible for Japan to accomplish this feat? Why were the Arabs incapable of it?

The Japanese had from the very start shown profound awareness of the nature of the western challenge on both the military-economic and the cultural-ideological levels.[1] The response to which this awareness gave rise expressed itself in a synthesis symbolized by the slogan: "eastern ethics and western science."[2]

Arab society lacked both Japan's concentrated awareness of the challenge and the eclectic propensity of the Japanese in meeting it. The Arab Awakening, which simultaneously aimed at achieving cultural rebirth and modernization, was unable to create the balance or to mark the fine limits achieved by the Japanese—i.e., to preserve traditional values and to adopt scientific techniques but, at the same time, avoid the contradictions inherent in this course of action. In the end it proved itself incapable of the synthesis which was at the basis of Japan's great triumph.

For the Islamic reformists—as well as for many Muslim secularists —the main task was to preserve Islamic values and to use them as the basis for a reform movement. But the crucial fact is that Islamic reformism failed to become the rallying point of the reform move-

---

[1] It must be admitted that Arab society, unlike the Japanese (for social, historical, and geopolitical reasons) did not form a unified whole which could be mobilized from a unified center of authority. It was crucial for the outcome of the Arab Awakening that it occurred amid social and territorial fragmentation enhanced and consolidated by expanding western imperialism.

[2] The Chinese We Yüan (1794–1856) advocated the same point: "Chinese learning to provide the [moral] basis, Western learning to provide the [technical] means." The Japanese, but not the Chinese nor the Arabs, lived up to this goal.

ment; on the contrary, it became the object of opposition of both the westernizing and the secularizing elements. Its efforts ossified, amid the mounting change, into rigid fundamentalist attitudes. Consequently, traditional values lost their relevance and were submerged.

Nor, on the other hand, could Islamic reformism achieve genuine solidarity with the conservative forces: Ottomanism and Islamism. A genuine Islamic conservatism capable of safeguarding the "eternal verities" and of preserving a core of loyalty within society likewise failed to develop. The conservative impulse of Islamic reformism found itself transformed into reaction.

Thus traditional values were not preserved; western science was not acquired.[3] Experience everywhere has shown that in cultural borrowing two things can be transmitted whole: finished goods and, within limits, the technical method of making them. What cannot be transmitted (but has to be absorbed and cultivated on a higher plane) are the constitutive elements of the scientific spirit—rational discipline, analytical observation, controlled procedures, criticism, realistic imagination, and self-correction.

The process of acquiring this spirit requires the systematic secularization of knowledge, which is the precondition of scientific thought. The reform movement in all its forms seemed incapable of achieving this secularization. It failed, in its main current, to disentangle the criteria of scientific truth from religious, political, and practical concerns and was consequently never able (except in rare instances by some Christian intellectuals) to achieve the level of genuine scientific consciousness. As long as intellectual discipline was not recognized in terms of its own proper values—i.e., as long as intellectual activity remained bound to political, religious, and practical considerations— the scientific mentality could not be genuinely acquired nor attain true autonomous existence. And without such existence, the scientific spirit could not become self-generating.[4]

Two processes, one social and the other psychological, further enhanced this situation. In Arab society, and in Muslim society

[3] Science is used here in the broadest designation of the term, as used, for example, by Karl Jaspers—"the art of distinguishing the real from the unreal, the factual from the fictitious, demonstrable knowledge from mere opinions, and objective certainty from subjective convictions." *Nietzsche,* trans. C. Wallraff and F. Schmitz (Tucson, Ariz., 1965), p. 30. But the term is also used to denote scientific theory and technique.

[4] Whitehead maintained, optimistically, that what the West could most readily supply to the nonwestern societies was "its science and scientific outlook," provided that the recipient was "a rational society"—which in this context is putting the cart before the horse. *Science in the Modern World,* Mentor ed., p. 11.

generally, the process of institutionalizing innovation always tended to express itself in formal and deliberate policies of cultural transplantations. Only where the groundwork was sufficiently developed did transplanting operations result in positive growth (e.g., military reform). In most areas—administrative, judicial, educational—the outcome was usually anemic, defective, and incomplete. Institutional reform was arbitrarily imposed from above and from the outside. Social forms and structures, as well as the notions and habits required for their preservation and development, were foreign imports—goods to be consumed, tools to be used. This only served to inhibit endogenous creativity and to speed up the corrosion of traditional institutions; it reflected, and was in turn reflected by, the discontinuity and disruptions which characterized social and intellectual transformation.

Internalization, which constituted the internal or subjective side of institutionalization, was beset by parallel shortcomings. It was impossible for an adaptive rationality to emerge (as happened in Japan) when a unitary collective orientation was absent. Fundamental values, both inherited and acquired, lacked not only a firm, external social base, but also the internal framework wherein they might be synthesized and incorporated into an integrated outlook. The tensions and convulsions characteristic of the Arab Awakening not only blocked the development of a coherent mental attitude but gave rise to widespread diffusion and divisiveness. This is one reason why, for example, Europe was always perceived out of focus. It was not possible either to protect oneself against its predatoriness nor to devise the proper method of acquiring its strength. The Arab Awakening, at its crucial turning point, was haunted by a sense of impotence and fear. Its leaders took to scapegoating.

The End of the Formative Phase

World War I brought to an end the first, formative phase of the Awakening and with it the beginnings of two radical shifts. First, the relative importance of the roles of the three main groups of Arab intellectuals underwent profound change. Secondly, the center of preoccupation shifted from the religious and intellectual spheres to the political—Europe now no longer appeared as western civilization but as western imperialism.

The Islamic reformists, who were at the center of the stage throughout most of the formative phase, began to retreat to the background. Though they still had an important role to play in the years to come, their dominant influence was broken. Indeed, by 1914

Islamic revivalism had run its course; nationalism and its demands, not the problems of Islamic reform, had become the central social force in both Egypt and the Fertile Crescent. The collapse of the Ottoman Empire and the abolition of the caliphate (1924) were catastrophic turning points for the Islamic reformists. The Arab revolt of 1916, sparked in the holy cities of the Hijaz and led by Muhammad's Hashimite descendants, represented the final betrayal of the "religious cause." Thus, for the Islamic reformists, the Allied victory of 1918, far from bringing liberation to the Arabs, was viewed as ushering in a period of general disintegration and collapse. It is not surprising that after the war the Wahhabi state of Ibn Saud appeared to many fervent Muslims to be the center of hope for Islam in the twentieth century.

After the war intellectual and social orientation shifted toward an irreversible westernizing and secularist direction. Religious authority, on both the social and political planes, decreased in the same proportion as the secular spirit spread. Islam, among the educated strata, was absorbed into secular ideology, where its influence is still most effective.

The position and role of the Christian intellectuals also underwent significant change after World War I. From the Christian standpoint the fall of the Ottoman Empire was welcomed as marking the end of "backwardness and oppression"; and the Allied victory as heralding the beginning of liberation.[5]

In the Fertile Crescent, with the establishment of the Anglo-French mandate, the relationship of Christian intellectualism to both secular and reformist Islam took a different form. In Lebanon Christian intellectualism began developing its own political and cultural framework; it soon began regarding itself as an extension of the "West," not in a vague cultural or religious sense but in a specific political sense. It conceived of itself as playing a new role in the surrounding Arab world as the "bridge" between (Arab) Islam and (Christian) Europe.

Gradually, the Christian intellectuals withdrew from the mainstream of Arab political and intellectual involvement. On the political level, Lebanon strove to consolidate a "neutral," noncommitted position; and on the cultural level, to cultivate a separate Lebanese identity resting on a Christian Lebanese mystique. In Egypt, where the most significant contributions of Christian intellectualism were

---

[5] Though typical, this view was not true of all Christians. Some, especially in Syria, identified themselves with Arab nationalism and threw their lot with Faysal and the nationalist group which had gathered around him in Damascus.

made in the formative phase of the Awakening, the importance of the Christian intellectuals waned. Cairo was no longer the center of feverish literary and intellectual activity. In the early 1920s this center shifted to New York where some of the most influential Christian writers of the interwar period joined together in the "literary guild" (*al-rabitah al-qalamiyyah*)[6] to produce some of the most important works of Arabic literature in the first half of the twentieth century. And Beirut gained new stature as a literary and cultural center, where a specifically Lebanese school of thought emerged. Significantly, French was adopted as the language of literary expression by a number of Lebanese writers,[7] and colloquial Lebanese Arabic was used as a serious medium of literature.

The group which now gained undisputed political ascendancy in both Egypt and the Fertile Crescent was the Muslim secularists. It now became, in Mosca's sense of the term, the "ruling class" in the Arab world. In Egypt this class formed itself around the Wafd party and the splinter blocs which broke away from it after 1922. In the Fertile Crescent it played its first important role in the kingdom of Damascus (1918–20); later it supplied the dominant leaders and politicians of the Anglo-French mandates of the Fertile Crescent.

Western Imperialism and Arab Modernization

By 1918 western (mainly British and French) imperialism had firmly established itself throughout the Arab world, except in Saudi Arabia and Yemen. From the standpoint of the colonized there is no such thing as good imperialism. Whatever form imperialism takes— direct colonization, political and economic imperialism, indirect control—it always exploits and deforms. Whatever good Egypt or the Fertile Crescent (or any other part of the Arab world) may have reaped from British or French rule it was always a by-product of a process designed to serve British and French interests. Western imperialism, despite certain positive aspects, was not a benevolent force in the Arab world; on the contrary, it was a force of social repression and economic manipulation. Even when Britain and France wished to

---

[6] Literally "the Pen League," with headquarters in lower Manhattan; some of these writers also wrote in English: Kahlil Gibran, Michael Nu'aymi, and Amin Rihani.

[7] French also became the language of daily life among French-educated Christians. The daily *L'Orient,* founded in Beirut in the early 1920s, is still probably the best French-language newspaper outside metropolitan France. Charles Kirm, George Shehadé, and others wrote exclusively in French and were published and read in France. English remained the language of North American emigrants and never took root in Christian Lebanon.

contribute to the welfare of their colonial wards, their efforts were severely limited not only by manpower and financial considerations, but by the irreducible, inherent conflict between ruler and ruled. Thus the modern projects introduced by imperialism—highways, railroads, port facilities, and administrative, educational, health, and agricultural institutions, etc.—could only be motivated by colonial economic, political and strategic interests. Of course, the view was that what was good for Europe was necessarily good for the natives. But imperialism, like the economic system which gave it impetus, evolved according to its own inner requirements, and, rooted in internal contradictions, it carried the seeds of its own disintegration. Before its final dissolution in the 1950s and 1960s, western imperialism had stamped its indelible mark on contemporary society.

1. Western imperialism was, in the first place, directly responsible for the political fragmentation of the Arab world in the twentieth century. An outstanding example of this was the balkanization of the Fertile Crescent by Britain and France. Every political boundary in the Arab world has been directly or indirectly drawn by western interests.

In economic as well as political terms, the creation of separate Arab sovereignties led not only to the polarization of power in the Arab world but also to the continued monopoly of oil—the Arab world's major natural resource—by patriarchal rulers and western oil cartels. During this critical period in which economic development should play a decisive role in the process of modernization it was possible to divert this vast resource into private hands and into foreign fields of investment.

2. Imperial and colonial domination also contributed to the fragmentation of the national movement into separate independent movements operating in the different political entities created by the western powers. Arab nationalism was thus reduced to several local sub-movements engaged in negative struggles against foreign rule. That key countries like Egypt, Syria, and Algeria were compelled, owing to foreign domination, to wage separate national struggles of independence was instrumental in blocking the normal evolution of a successful united-Arab movement after independence had been secured.

3. Western imperialism was by its very nature compelled to carry out policies and to assume attitudes that were inimical to certain forms of social change. This trend was particularly strong in the colonized areas, such as Algeria, Libya and Palestine, which were directly colonized by French, Italian, and Zionist settlers, and where the Arab population was physically uprooted and subjected to legal,

social, and political discrimination. In all dominated areas, whether domination took a colonial, imperialistic, or indirect political form, the dominating power followed a course of action which helped to disrupt internal political integration and to inhibit indigenous economic development.

4. On the social level, western imperialism contributed to retarding modernization by its repressive social policies. It actively encouraged ethnic and religious differences and strengthened regional separatism. It backed the conservative and reactionary social groups and cemented class and economic distinctions. It contributed to the consolidation of the power and privileges of the large landlords, the tribal shaykhs, the conservative clergy, and the import-oriented merchant and business class. It cultivated moderate, native politicians and used them to maintain and extend its power.

5. On a purely economic level imperial domination was responsible for arresting the growth of indigenous capitalistic formations in the Arab world.[8] Native capital, and the class that would have utilized it, was diverted into other functions more in harmony with western economic and social interests. The socioeconomic formations with which Arab society was "pregnant" were aborted at an early stage of development, constituting a serious setback to the process of economic modernization.

6. The psychological impact of western imperialism and colonization, particularly on the younger generation, was profound and incalculable in its effects. By controlling education it tried to influence the intellectual and political orientation of the younger generation. On a more general level, western domination gave rise to a feeling of inferiority and frustration which often expressed itself in nihilism and despair. Western rule, supported by the tacit or active collaboration of the older generation, served further to widen the gap between the generations and to create a humiliated, rebellious youth.[9] It is this generation which in the mid-twentieth century finally revolted not only against imperialistic Europe, but also against the Europe of "western culture." The repudiation which this revolt signified has been expressed in the words of one of the Arab world's leading young

[8] This point is analyzed in depth in Maxim Rodinson, *Islam et Capitalisme* (Paris, 1967), pp. 134–47.

[9] See, for example, Malik Bennabi's remarks (himself a member of the educated North African generation that experienced this humiliation): "L'occident n'emporte pas ses vertus hors de 'son' monde. Hors de ses frontières maternelles, il n'est plus 'l'homme' mais 'l'Européen.' Et il ne voit plus des hommes mais 'des indigènes.'" *L'Afro-Asiatisme* (Cairo, 1956), p. 36.

poets: "We no longer believe in Europe. We no longer have faith in its political system or in its philosophies. Worms have eaten into its social structure as they have into . . . its very soul. Europe for us—we backward, ignorant, impoverished people—is a corpse."[10]

[10] Ahmad 'Ali Sa'id (Adonis), *Lisan al-Hal* (May 7, 1967).

Index

'Abboud, Maroun, 4
'Abdu, Muhammad, 5, 13–14, 24–29,
  34–40, 45, 49, 52, 62, 71–72, 79,
  92–95
Abdul Hamid, 4–5, 9, 14, 47, 58, 71,
  103, 108, 122
al-Afghani, Jamal al-Din, 5, 9, 13,
  24–29, 32, 35, 38–43, 48, 51–52,
  72, 78–79, 98, 109–10, 112
al-'Ahd. See Covenant
Amin, Qasim, 88, 92–97, 101, 104
al-Antaki, 'Abd al-Masih, 15
Antun, Farah, 53, 66, 70–79, 84–86,
  91, 93
Arab Awakening, 1, 3, 14, 22, 27,
  66, 92, 129, 131, 133
Arab Congress, 124
Arabic, language, 11, 14, 55, 65, 109,
  115, 125; literature, 17
Arabism, 64
Arab (Hashemite) Revolt, 89, 111,
  121, 132
Arslan, Shakib, 51, 88, 110, 123
atheism, 74
Atiyah, Edward, 54, 120–21
Austro-Hungarian Empire, 18
Averöes. See Ibn Rushd
al-Azhar, 25, 40
al-'Azm, Rafiq, 88
'Azma, 98–99
Azoury, Najib, 118

Bacon, Francis, 71
Bentham, Jeremy, 68
Blanc, Louis, 68
Bolshevism, 50, 86
Le Bon, Gustave, 68
Bonald, Louis de, 68
British occupation of Egypt, 4, 15,
  38, 46
Büchner, Ludwig, 69, 71, 81
al-Bustani, Butrus, 53, 58, 64–65, 70,
  80–81, 91, 115, 119
al-Bustani, Salim, 53, 57–58, 66

al-Bustani, Sulayman, 53, 58, 62,
  115–17

caliphate, 12–15, 21, 36, 61, 109, 123,
  125, 132
Campanella, Tommaso, 70
Cheikho, Louis, 53
Circassians, 122
Committee of Union and Progress
  (C.U.P.), 124
Comte, Auguste, 68–69, 71, 75, 93
Constant, Benjamin, 68
Covenant, 127
crusades, 47

al-Dallal, Jubra'il, 61
dar al-Islam. See Muslim community
Darwinism, 45, 56, 66, 68–69, 93
decentralization, 18, 21, 118
determinism, 33
Durkheim, Emile, 75

elite, 75, 83
the Enlightenment, 54, 66
europeanization, 90, 98

Fabianism, 83
fatherland, 64, 119
fundamentalism, 22

Ghanim, Khalil, 58, 81
al-Ghazzali, 11, 25
Gibran, Kahlil, 67, 133
gradualism, 62
Gramsci, Antonio, 1
Greek Orthodox, 14, 16, 52, 113–14

Haddad, Niqula, 53, 84, 91
hadith, 11, 103
Haykal, Muhammad Husayn, 88
historicism, 6
holy war, 47, 109
humanism, 17
al-Humsi, Qistaki, 53